*Lake District
Mountain Landforms*

Lake District Mountain Landforms

Peter Wilson

For my Mother –
for her love and devotion

For Frances –
for sharing many days

For Richard (Dick) Clark (1927–2009) and
Peter Vincent (1944–2009) –
geomorphologists and friends

Copyright © Peter Wilson 2010

First published in 2010 on behalf of the author by
Scotforth Books, Lancaster
www.scotforthbooks.com
www.carnegiepublishing.com

ISBN 13: 978-1-904244-56-1

Printed in the UK by Butler Tanner & Dennis, Somerset

Contents

Preface

MY INTEREST IN THE COUNTRYSIDE was stimulated whilst a schoolboy in Nelson, Lancashire. On three or four occasions in the 1960s my year group at Barrowford School were taken to Whitehough Camp School, Barley, at the foot of Pendle Hill. Under the direction of Whitehough's headmaster, Kenneth Oldham, and his staff we ranged over and around Pendle as well as further afield into the Ribble Valley and Yorkshire Dales. We hiked across hills and moors, descended into the depths of limestone potholes and cave systems, and spent nights under canvas. Usually we got wet, dirty, cold and windswept. We carried large and heavy rucksacks. You either loved it or loathed it.

Later, as a geography student at Salford University, I was introduced to geology and geomorphology by lecturers Peter Vincent and Colin Harrison and came to realise that the landscape that had excited me as a youngster had an interesting story to tell. Suddenly, hill walking took on an added dimension.

Although I had walked in the Lake District before starting at university it was whilst I was an undergraduate that I began to go there regularly. The university Hill-walking Club organised weekends in youth hostels (Eskdale was my first) and another lecturer, Keith Grime, had access to the Rucksack Club hut at Seathwaite in Dunnerdale, and each term a group of us went there for a weekend. For several years my university vacations were spent as a leader of hill-walking groups for CHA (Countrywide Holidays Association) at their centres in Eskdale, Grasmere, Ambleside, and Borrowdale.

It was through working for CHA that I met Frances, who later became my wife. She also enjoys hill walking and has been tolerant of numerous geomorphological diversions on the way and my absences for fieldwork.

Shortly after taking up a post at the New University of Ulster I met Richard (Dick) Clark. I was in the School of Biological and Environmental Sciences, Dick was in the School of Education but our mutual interests in landforms led to collaborative research. Unfortunately our first efforts remain unpublished. Nevertheless, following his retirement and move to Hartsop we pursued research into the origins of Lake District landforms. On numerous occasions Dick, and his wife Liz, welcomed me into their home, and I benefited enormously from the fieldwork and discussions we shared over more than twenty years.

Now, having had a number of academic articles about Lake District landforms published (several jointly with Dick), a book on the same theme seems a logical progression. However, this book would never have come about had the people mentioned above not been willing to share their knowledge of the countryside and their time with me.

Peter Wilson
Portstewart
New Year 2010

Acknowledgements

I AM INDEBTED TO MANY PEOPLE, namely Frances Wilson, Ian Brodie, Dee Lacy, Bernie Lafferty, Tony Rogers, Alan Smith, and Peter Vincent, who read either the whole manuscript or selected chapters and suggested various improvements, and Kilian McDaid and Lisa Rodgers, at the University of Ulster, who prepared the diagrams for publication. 2.2 is reproduced by permission of the British Geological Survey (© NERC 2009. All rights reserved. IPR/119–61CT); Brian Wilkinson of Keswick supplied 7.32a and Sandra Sáenz-López Pérez and Chet Van Duzer kindly allowed me to use 7.32b; Sabine Skae at the Dock Museum, Barrow-in Furness, provided 9.1b; 10.2 is adapted from a diagram in *Hostile Habitats* (Scottish Mountaineering Trust, 2006) and is published here with the approval of John Gordon.

Any errors or omissions remain the responsibility of the author.

Preamble

THE LAKE DISTRICT IS ONE of the best-known and most popular areas in Britain. For over two hundred years it has attracted visitors. Without a doubt the nature of this attraction is the landscape. Not only has the Lake District attracted visitors it has also inspired visitors and residents alike – for example, the landscape painters Turner and Constable, the poets Wordsworth and Coleridge, and the children's writers Beatrix Potter and Arthur Ransome. It has also become one of Britain's foremost areas for upland recreation (hill walking, climbing, fell running, mountain biking, hang- and para-gliding) and it inspired Alfred Wainwright into producing his, now iconic, guidebooks to the fells.

No other area of Britain has had as many books written about it as the Lake District. So, why is another one needed?

The simple answer is that a non-specialist book dealing with mountain landforms has not yet been written even though these landforms underpin the character of the Lake District landscape.

Many of the books devoted to the Lake District, irrespective of their general theme, comment on the splendour of the landscape and proffer, at most, a token gesture to the contribution that landforms make to that landscape. Usually a brief account of the geology is followed by statements to the effect that the Lake District has been glaciated in the recent past. However, the Lake District has much more to it than the imprint of glaciation alone. There are numerous locations where features associated with periglacial processes (those dominated by repeated freezing and thawing), hillslope activity, and river action can be seen. Some of these features are being created today; others are relict and date from times when environmental conditions were different from those of the present. These all contribute to the special character of the landscape we enjoy.

My use of the term 'mountain landforms' is not restricted to features occurring above a particular height; rather it refers to features that are found in the mountainous part of the Lake District. Thus, landforms of valley floor, mountaintop and areas in-between are included.

The intention of this book is to provide descriptions and explanations by text, simple line diagrams and photographs of the great array of landforms that exists in the Lake District. Landform characteristics are portrayed and the processes that created them are outlined. Some consideration is also given to the age of the various features. Details of specific and easily accessible classic landforms are provided in the various chapters. In doing all this I hope to demonstrate that there is much more to the Lake District than, to quote an unknown source, 'nowt but stanes and watter'.

Landforms vary enormously in size and shape; some are created by the weathering and erosion of rock and others result from the deposition of materials. With regard to depositional landforms, the description and interpretation of their sediment composition are not considered in detail here because in many cases these materials are not exposed. The best way to recognise and appreciate the variety of Lake District landforms is to go out and see them. Observation is an integral part of landform interpretation; the same experience cannot be gained by simply reading and looking at the pictures and diagrams in this book – although it is a good place to begin!

This is not intended as an academic text, nor is it intended as a guidebook. It aims to bridge the gap between the two by providing enthusiastic visitors to the Lake District, particularly those who go fell walking, with explanations of how and when the landforms were created. The book will also be of value to teachers and students of geography and geology who visit the Lake District for field study courses.

Have you ever wondered why Skiddaw is different from Helvellyn, or why the east side of the Helvellyn range is different from its west side, or why Scafell Pike has numerous boulders and High Street does not, or why Wast Water is different from Windermere, or how the passes were made, or why the summit of Helm Crag is, well, a bit craggy? If so, this book will assist your understanding. Even if you have not asked yourself these questions don't despair – you can still become an authority – just look around as you walk. Take in the big picture of the stunning landscape – perhaps the view down Great Langdale as you sit at the summit of Bowfell – then try to see the various components that make up that view: the boulders around the summit, the steep slopes that sweep down to Mickleden below Pike o'Stickle, the low col that leads via Blea Tarn to Little Langdale, the twisting form and flat floor of Great Langdale and so on. You are beginning to see the pieces of the jigsaw.

Alternatively, on any walk taken in the Lake District a plethora of landforms will be encountered so try to identify them next time you are there. If you start from Seathwaite in Borrowdale and go by Stockley Bridge and Styhead to the summit of Great Gable and then return to Seathwaite by going over Green Gable, Brandreth and Grey Knotts to Honister Pass you will meet with the following landforms – glacial troughs, hanging valleys, cirques, roches moutonnées, moraines, erratics, screes, blockfields, tors, fan-deltas, tarns, terracettes, floodplains, a rock-cut river channel, and a braided gravel-bed channel. Many of these landforms would be seen if you only walked from Seathwaite to Styhead Pass and back. If these features don't mean much to you at present then this book will explain them so that next time you walk in the Lake District you will know what to look out for and be able to impress you friends with your new found knowledge of the landscape.

I believe that a fuller appreciation of any area can be obtained by seeking and gaining some understanding of its cultural and natural history. Because landforms are part of nature, some knowledge of how they formed and when they were created adds another dimension to time spent in the fell country. I trust this book will enable you to derive enjoyment from recognising and understanding the landforms – the **geomorphology** – of an area often regarded as the 'jewel in the crown' of upland landscapes – the Lake District National Park.

CHAPTER ONE

Introduction

Geomor ... what??

THE LAKE DISTRICT NATIONAL PARK is a small and compact area of less than 2,500 km^2 in northwest England consisting of rugged mountains, shapely hills, deep pastoral valleys containing mixed woodland and scattered settlements, and numerous lakes and tarns. It is one of several areas within Great Britain to have been accorded the status of National Park, and to anyone familiar with the region the justification for this designation is immediately apparent. Of the 12 million visitors attracted to the Lake District each year a significant proportion probably go there because of the outstanding landscape. In essence the attraction is the physical landscape, and this comprises an assemblage of landforms. The study and appreciation of landforms, their origins and their age is known as **geomorphology**. Unbeknown to many of the visitors it is the geomorphology of the Lake District that has taken them there.

Geomorphology is the scientific study of the Earth's landforms and the processes responsible for their development. Those who study geomorphology are known as **geomorphologists** and concern themselves with explaining how landforms evolve. In doing this they have to take into account variations in rock type and in climate, and the interactions that occur between these phenomena in different regions and over different timescales.

Traditionally geomorphology is a branch of Physical Geography, and students who take A-level Geography and then go on to read Geography at university usually receive a thorough grounding in the subject. In addition, students of Geology, Environmental Science, and Civil Engineering are also exposed to courses that explore the surface processes and landforms of the Earth.

1.1 Great Langdale and the Langdale Pikes. Views like this are rightly accepted as representing stunning mountain landscape, but what is sometimes not appreciated is that the scene is made up of several distinctive geomorphological features. When you have finished the book you should be able to return to this picture, recognise individual landforms and, hopefully, understand how and when they formed.

Although geomorphology is often seen as a purely academic discipline, it has real world applications. The roads on which we drive, the buildings in which we live and work, and the fields on which we depend for agricultural produce are all influenced by geomorphology. Furthermore, concerns about global warming and climate change have brought landforms to wider public attention. In particular the greater incidence of storms and torrential rainfall along with rising temperatures has captured media attention. Pictures of floods, landslides, avalanches and rapidly shrinking glaciers and ice-sheets appear regularly in television news broadcasts. There is now a greater public perception of how and why the Earth's surface undergoes change and a growing appreciation that the surface is dynamic rather than a static backdrop to life, industry and recreation.

However, geomorphology is not an exact science and for some landforms there is disagreement amongst the subject's practitioners as to just how the formative processes operated and therefore how the landforms were created. To overcome such problems many geomorphologists have adopted from geology the practical dictum that **'the present is the key**

to the past'. In other words, processes that operate at the present time are assumed to be the same as those that operated in the past and by understanding contemporary processes we can explain relict landforms. But not all geomorphologists would agree with that! There is also the issue of **equifinality**. This refers to the fact that different processes may produce similar landforms. For example, an accumulation of scree on a steep hillside may have resulted from the fall of boulders caused by alternate freezing and thawing of water that had percolated into the joints on the rock-face above the scree; on the other hand the scree may have been produced by earth tremors that caused the fall of loosened rock. In the case of scree, it is not always easy to tell what caused it to accumulate.

Collectively, the landforms of an area constitute the local topography or physical landscape. In some areas people admire landscape and protect it from over-exploitation and degradation by declaring it a National Park. These areas are judged to be of high landscape quality and have often been the focus of detailed geomorphological study. Such studies have given rise to an alternative definition of geomorphology as **'the science of scenery'** (1.1).

A little bit of history

The term 'geomorphology' was first used in the 1870s and has been in widespread use since 1900. It is therefore one of the younger scientific disciplines. However, between 2,000 and 2,500 years ago Greek philosophers wrote about river valleys and mountains, and speculated as to how they had come into being. Herodotus and Aristotle considered various aspects of the Earth's surface and only pedants would dispute their conclusions regarding relationships between the land and the sea. Much later, Leonardo da Vinci wrote about the formation of valleys, erosion and deposition, and explained the occurrence of fossil marine shells in mountains as a consequence of changes in the levels of the land and the sea.

Modern scientific geomorphology is often said to have begun in the last decade of the nineteenth century through the work of the American geographer William Morris Davis. He proposed that landscapes evolve through stages of youth, maturity and old age, and termed this the 'geographical cycle'. Davis had been influenced by Charles Darwin's theory of biological evolution and thought landscapes should follow a similar pattern of development. Although the 'geographical cycle' has since been shown to be an over simplification of reality, it formed a base from which scientific enquiry could proceed and is often regarded as being the stimulus that encouraged the pursuit of a greater understanding of landform and landscape development.

Over the years the Lake District has had its fair share of geomorphologists but the people listed below would not have considered themselves as such. Indeed, some of them lived, and had died, well before the word 'geomorphology' was coined. Nevertheless, as commentators on the Lake District scene they were influenced by the physical landscape, and the recognition of landforms and some of the processes that shape the surface are evident in their writings. This goes to prove that, although we may not realise it, there is a little bit of the geomorphologist in many of us!

Thomas West's *Guide to the Lakes*, published in 1778, was the first important guidebook to the Lake District. He recommended that tourists visit a series of viewpoints or 'stations' from which to view the scenery. One of his stations was Castle Crag in Borrowdale from where he drew attention to the line taken by the River Derwent, the islands in Derwent Water, and the contrast between the flat ground beyond Keswick and the abrupt slopes rising towards Skiddaw. West was pointing out diversity in the physical landscape of the Lake District. Today, we can offer geomorphological explanations for these features. West also suggested that, at his stations, tourists should view the scenery by turning their back to the view and look into a 'landscape mirror' of plano-convex glass. This rather strange action was considered to provide a more pleasing, if somewhat scaled-down and less 'terrible' perspective of the dramatic mountain terrain.

Another influential guidebook to the Lakes was that by William Wordsworth. First published in 1810 it described the topography of each of the main valleys. Such was its success that it went through several editions and the later ones included sections on geology. The 1853 edition for example, published three years after Wordsworth's death, included five geological letters written by Professor Adam Sedgwick of Cambridge University. Guidebook writers and their publishers were beginning to realise that they had a duty to interpret the physical landscape for the benefit of their readers.

During the twentieth century the distinctly different writing styles of A. Harry Griffin and Alfred Wainwright have extolled the virtues of the Lake District landscape. Both have documented the fell country and their wanderings through it in great detail. Griffin's prose reflects the personal experiences gained over many years of walking, climbing and ski-ing, and demonstrates an intimacy with the landscape that few have matched. His descriptions of individual fells reveal an acute awareness of the terrain and its dynamic character.

1.2 Wythburn has a reputation for being excessively wet underfoot. The stream meanders through a large area of bog that has developed across sites of former tarns.

1.3 The well-known rock outcrops on the summit of Helm Crag and the adjacent hummocky and boulder-strewn terrain are the result of a landslip that caused the eastern (right-hand) side of the ridge to move a short distance downslope.

The Wainwright guidebooks with their hand-drawn maps, sketches and panoramas, and the factual notes and humorous personal touches, have brought the landscape alive for the thousands who now follow in his footsteps. Wainwright devoted space and comment to many landforms alongside or near the paths. For example, in Book 3 *The Central Fells*, there are numerous references to geomorphological features – the split boulder of Blea Rigg, the Bowder Stone, boulder scree and rock towers (tors) of Grange Fell, the moraines of Greenup Gill, the peat bogs (former tarns) of Wythburn (1.2), and the Helm Crag landslip and the distinctive summit-ridge rock outcrops of that fell (1.3). But having said that, there are several examples of geomorphological features that he didn't document in spite of their prominence on the fell sides.

As well as these eminent Lake District devotees there have been many for whom geomorphology was either a part of their professional work or a principal activity occupying their retirement years. Of these, Clifton Ward (1843–1880) falls into the first category and Thomas Hay (1873–1957) into the latter.

Ward's contribution to Lake District geomorphology came through his work for the Geological Survey. He was sent to the Lake District in 1868 to conduct mapping of the rock types and their structures in the northern part of the area. This he did with great effectiveness but he also considered the relationships between the landscape and the geology and devoted much of his energy to the issue, prevalent at that time, of whether the local glacial phenomena were the product of land-based ice or could be accounted for by floating ice (see Chapter 4). Ward favoured the latter idea and wrote extensively of the supporting evidence that he had acquired. He also commented on the ability of streams and rivers to transport sediment from upper to lower reaches of valleys and how this material contributed to the 'filling up of lakes' (see Chapter 7). On several mountains, including the summit ridge of Helm Crag, he identified and described prominent rock fissures that he surmised were the result of ancient earthquake shocks (see Chapter 6).

Between 1926 and 1951 Thomas Hay was author of thirteen papers on aspects of Lake District geomorphology (although he preferred to use the terms 'topography' and 'physiography'). Most of these contributions were researched, written and published during his retirement years at Moss Crag, Glenridding. Although he ranged widely in the Lake District the Ullswater valley and its surrounding fells provided the locations for many of his studies. He concentrated on the erosional and depositional evidence for former glaciation (see Chapter 4), on the effects produced by contemporary freezing and thawing of the soil (see Chapter 5) and on features occurring along lake shorelines (see Chapter 7). Floods and flooding were also detailed and, like Ward before him and Wainwright after him, the Helm Crag landslip came in for description and consideration. Hay also recorded the first British examples of gliding blocks (now known as ploughing boulders – see Chapter 5) that are particularly common on some fell sides. His map showing the distribution of glacial landforms in the Ullswater valley, published in 1934, has not yet been surpassed. For an amateur working in retirement his contribution to Lake District geomorphology was enormous. As new ideas gain ground and old ones are rejected it is testimony to Hay's observations that his work continues to be cited in the geomorphological literature.

Many other people, too numerous to mention here, have contributed descriptions and explanations of Lake District landforms. The list of Further Reading at the end of this book gives their names and details of the type of studies they have undertaken.

Landform age and how we know

Many techniques exist that enable geomorphologists to establish the age of landforms. But why should we want to know how old the landforms are? Is it of any value to know?

In the Lake District different processes have created different landforms at different times. Knowing when these features developed is fundamental to understanding landscape history. Having a handle on landform age tells us about past processes and times of environmental change. By determining age it becomes possible to build up a chronological sequence of landshaping events. In other words, we can interpret and reconstruct the history of the landscape.

Perhaps the simplest way of all to date the landforms of an area is to put them into a relative age sequence. This entails looking at the relationships between different features and trying to ascertain their age order – youngest to oldest – and follows the **principal of stratigraphic superposition** which states that in a sequence of deposits the lower strata are older than the upper strata. To illustrate this we may think of a series of valley-side **moraine ridges** created by a long-vanished glacier. The moraines may have been covered in part by **scree** from hillside cliffs. Similar moraines on the valley floor may have been buried in part by **alluvium** deposited by the river. In both cases the moraines (lower strata) are clearly older than the materials that partly obscure them; or to put it another way, both the scree and the alluvium (upper strata) are younger than the moraines (1.4). However, in this example we are not able to say whether the scree is younger or older than the alluvium because these materials are not in mutual contact and therefore do not display a direct stratigraphic relationship. Other techniques that provide absolute (numerical) ages would be required to resolve that issue.

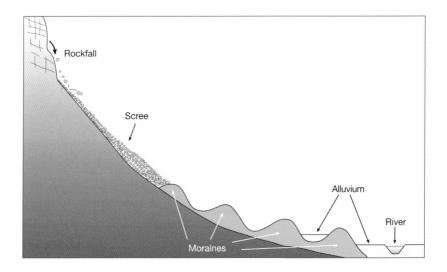

1.4 Moraines, scree and alluvium – assessment of their stratigraphic relationships makes it possible to place them in relative age sequence.

Numerical ages for landforms can be obtained in several ways. Some of these techniques are rather specialised and expensive to apply, others are less so. Furthermore, the time spans covered vary with the method. An extremely valuable source of information is documentary evidence – written records, maps and photographs. Documentary sources are particularly useful for the last 100 years or so and can provide details about landscape changes such as those brought about by flooding and rockfall activity (1.5). The further back in time we go the less reliable the documentary evidence becomes – if it is available at all. Then we have to adopt other means of dating the landforms.

Of the many specialised techniques that provide numerical ages just three are mentioned below. These are the ones that have the greatest potential to inform us about landform age in the Lake District and are termed **lichenometry**, **radiocarbon dating** and **cosmogenic-isotope dating**. With all these methods it needs to be remembered that they can only be applied if the correct materials are available and even then there is a degree of uncertainty associated with each.

1.5 Information about rockfalls at Deer Bield Crag in Far Easedale is documented in climbing guidebooks. Some of these boulders came down in 1997 when a buttress collapsed, including the gigantic one leaning against the base of the crag.

- **Lichenometry** or **lichenometric dating** relies on the growth rate of lichen on rock surfaces. When rock surfaces are exposed as a result of erosion or deposition they may be colonised by lichen. The greenish-yellow *Rhizocarpon geographicum* (Map lichen) is commonly used for dating in geomorphology because it is widespread, conspicuous, and tends to grow at a steady rate (1.6). If the rate of growth can be determined by measuring lichen size on surfaces of known date (e.g. buildings, gravestones) then the sizes of lichen on landforms of unknown age may provide an indication of when that surface became available for colonisation – i.e. its age. In certain situations the technique can be used for dating surfaces up to about 500 years old. After that time individual lichen start to merge and their growth is restricted so that they are unsuitable for surface age estimation. Although lichens have been used since the 1950s for dating landforms, there are only a few instances of the technique being applied in the Lake District. Specifically, scree slopes and boulders deposited by river floods have been investigated. Big rockfalls within the last few hundred years would also be prime candidates for age assessment using lichens.

1.6 By measuring lichen size (diameter) and by knowing the rate at which lichens grow on boulders it may be possible to establish when some flood and rockfall debris was deposited. The scale bar divisions are 5 cm.

- **Radioactive carbon** (^{14}C) occurs in the carbon dioxide of the atmosphere and is added to plant and animal tissues as a result of life processes. When an organism dies it stops accumulating ^{14}C and as a result of radioactive decay the ^{14}C begins to decrease. Because the level of ^{14}C in living organisms is known and because the rate of radioactive decay is also known, the amount of ^{14}C remaining in decomposing tissue is a measure of the time that has passed since the death of the organism. Where plant and animal tissues are fortuitously preserved due to burial by sediments they may yield age estimates not only for time of death but also for time of burial. The ^{14}C technique is valuable over a time span of about 200 to 60,000 years; after that time the amount of ^{14}C remaining in tissue is extremely small and impossible to measure. In the Lake District the ^{14}C technique has been applied to layers of peat that have been buried by sediments deposited by rivers and by hill-slope processes (1.7) in order to establish the age of those landforms created by sediment accumulation.
- **Cosmogenic-isotope dating** is based on the principle that cosmic radiation bombards the Earth continuously and interacts with soil and rock surfaces to produce cosmogenic isotopes (radioactive elements) in those materials. The rates at which the isotopes are produced are known, so that a measure of their concentration provides an estimate of the time over which the material has been exposed to the radiation. The method is especially suited to dating the exposure time (age) of rock landforms or depositional landforms with an abundance of large boulders on their surfaces (1.8). Timescales covered by the technique range from thousands to millions of years. In the Lake District the method has been applied

1.7 Radiocarbon (^{14}C) dating can be used to determine the age of peat at different positions in sequences like this and so determine the times at which the interbedded layers of sand and gravel were deposited. The scale bar divisions are 5 cm.

1.8 Large boulders sitting on moraines are amenable to cosmogenic-isotope dating. The survey pole divisions are 20 cm.

to landforms associated with glaciation – **roches moutonnées** and moraines.

In spite of these absolute dating techniques being available, most of the landforms in the Lake District do not, as yet, have absolute ages assigned to them. This is particularly true of the suite of glacial landforms. These features are generally attributed to the last two episodes of glaciation that affected the landscape between about 30,000 and 12,000 years ago. This association of landforms with a particular climate at a particular time is known as **climatic correlation** – the landforms are correlated with global climatic changes whose ages have been determined from studies undertaken elsewhere in the world.

CHAPTER TWO

The geology of the Lake District

Introduction

IT IS VERY USEFUL to have some knowledge of the geology of the Lake District in order to better understand why the landforms look like they do. Different types of rock respond in different ways and at different rates to the various processes of weathering and erosion (denudation), and this accounts for much of the variation we can see in the physical landscape. Properties such as hardness, mineral composition, porosity, permeability, grain size and the extent to which the grains are cemented together determine the level of resistance of a particular rock to the agents of physical and chemical weathering.

Three broad groupings of rock, based on how they formed, are recognised by geologists. These are termed: **igneous**, **sedimentary**, and **metamorphic**; examples of all three rock types can be found in the Lake District.

- **Igneous** rocks are those formed by the cooling and solidification of molten magma. They comprise lava flows that were extruded on to the Earth's surface and cooled quickly resulting in grains (crystals) of small size, and magma bodies that were intruded into the crust but because they did not reach the surface they cooled slowly and this allowed large crystals to develop. Basalt and andesite are examples of the former, granite and gabbro examples of the latter. Distinctions between types of extrusive and types of intrusive igneous rocks are based on their content of silica (SiO_2).

- **Sedimentary** rocks are divided into three groups: (1) accumulations of rock particles and minerals that have been weathered and eroded from pre-existing rocks, deposited and cemented, are known as **clastic** or **detrital** sedimentary rocks and examples include sandstones and shales; (2) **organic** sedimentary rocks, such as coal, form from the build up of plant and animal tissues; (3) the precipitation of mineral material out of water gives rise to **chemical** sedimentary rocks such as some limestones. A characteristic feature of sedimentary rocks is that they exhibit layering (bedding).

- **Metamorphic** rocks develop as a result of physical and chemical transformations to pre-existing igneous and sedimentary rocks. The changes are brought about by temperature and pressure increases that are sufficient to cause recrystallization of the minerals. Examples include slate (from shale), quartzite (from sandstone) and marble (from limestone).

In general terms, igneous and metamorphic rocks are resistant to denudation. On the other hand, sedimentary rocks vary in their ability to withstand denudation mainly because of the variations in the basic properties listed in the first paragraph. Therefore landform variations across an area can often be accounted for partly by differences in the underlying rock types.

Another important geological influence on the landforms of an area is the rock structures. In some cases structures may dictate where and how denudation operates and be the dominant factor in explaining landform development. Structures include folds, faults, and joints. Geological mapping in the Lake District over many years by numerous individuals has demonstrated an abundance of these features at a range of scales. It can and will be shown in the pages that follow that some landforms owe their existence to geological structures that have been exploited by the agents of denudation.

Beginnings and pioneers

Scientific descriptions of Lake District rocks started in the early years of the nineteenth century. The first geological account of the district is credited to the Keswick clock and watch repairer, and local guide, Jonathan Otley (1766–1856). In 1820 he had published a short article in both *The Lonsdale Magazine* and *The Philosophical Magazine* in which he outlined his views on the division of Lake District rocks. Three years later he published a guidebook for tourists to the Lake District and included a chapter on the geology. His book went through nine editions, the last being in 1857, and with the passage of time he developed and expanded upon his geological ideas and observations.

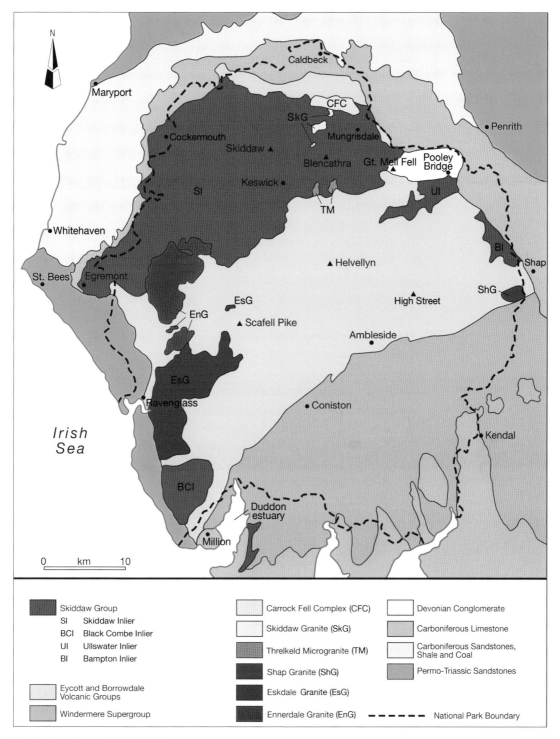

2.1 Geological map of the Lake District.

Skiddaw Group
SI   Skiddaw Inlier
BCI   Black Combe Inlier
UI   Ullswater Inlier
BI   Bampton Inlier

Eycott and Borrowdale
Volcanic Groups

Windermere Supergroup

Carrock Fell Complex (CFC)

Skiddaw Granite (SkG)

Threlkeld Microgranite (TM)

Shap Granite (ShG)

Eskdale Granite (EsG)

Ennerdale Granite (EnG)

Devonian Conglomerate

Carboniferous Limestone

Carboniferous Sandstones,
Shale and Coal

Permo-Triassic Sandstones

- - - - - National Park Boundary

However, knowledge of the variations in Lake District rocks goes back many, many years before Otley's time. Some 6,000 years ago, during the Neolithic period, small-scale quarrying was taking place on Pike o'Stickle. Axe heads were fashioned from the rocks for local use but were also traded widely. During the Roman occupation slates were quarried and used for roofing of the forts at Ambleside and Hardknott. The use of slate for roofing ceased following the Roman withdrawal but was later revived and several quarries, producing facing stones, flagstones, and ornamental pieces, as well as slates, remain in operation. There are numerous small, disused and overgrown quarries on the fellsides that testify to the local importance attained by this industry. In Elizabethan times the mining of metal ores was developed. German miners were employed and the main centres of extraction were around Newlands, Coniston and Caldbeck.

Nevertheless, Otley's work laid the foundations on which numerous subsequent studies could and would build and in 1916 to acknowledge his valuable contribution to the discipline, John Marr a Cambridge professor termed him the 'Father of Lakeland Geology'. Adam Sedgwick (1785–1873), Clifton Ward (1843–1880) and John Marr (1857–1933) were also major players in the story of Lake District geology as have been many other individuals, several of whom were, and some still are, employed by the British Geological Survey. Those wanting to learn more about these pioneers and the work they undertook are advised to read Alan Smith's *The Rock Men: Pioneers of Lakeland Geology* (Cumberland Geological Society, 2001). It is the work of these people that has resulted in the geological map of the Lake District that we have today (2.1).

The rock groups

Otley identified several distinctive rock groups and although other geologists have since expended a considerable amount of research time and effort his basic sub-division has stood the test of detailed scrutiny. Some refinements to the scheme have been made and the terminology has changed but Otley's observations are recognisable in the modern geological map.

The Lake District is underlain by a series of old hard rocks that at different times have been elevated by forces acting on the Earth's crust. Periods of uplift were followed by weathering and erosion, which reduced the terrain to lower levels. Younger rocks, which once covered the old hard rocks, have been stripped away and are now found around the margins of

Period	Age (m. yr.)	Rock types/groups (environment)	Igneous intrusions	Major events
Quaternary	2.6–present	Products of glacial, periglacial, fluvial and mass movement processes		Glaciation
Tertiary	65–2.6	Not present		
Cretaceous	145–65	Not present		
Jurassic	200–145	Not present		
Triassic	250–200	New Red Sandstone (St. Bees) (subaerial)		
Permian	300–250	New Red Sandstone (Vale of Eden) (subaerial)		
				Hercynian Orogeny
Carboniferous	360–300	Sandstones, shale and coal (West Cumbria) (delta/swamp) Limestone (Caldbeck, Shap, Kendal) (marine)		
Devonian	415–360	Conglomerate (Mell Fells) (subaerial)	Shap Skiddaw	
				Caledonian Orogeny
Silurian	440–415	Windermere Supergroup (marine)		
Ordovician	490–440	Borrowdale Volcanic Group (subaerial) Skiddaw Group (marine)	Threlkeld Eskdale Ennerdale Carrock Fell	
Cambrian	540–490	Not present		
Pre-Cambrian	Before 540	Not present		

m. yr. millions of years

Table 2.1 Lake District rocks and events in relation to the geological timescale.

the district (2.2). As far as this book is concerned the 'important' rocks are the three groups that occupy most of the area and trend broadly west-southwest to east-northeast. From north to south these are the Skiddaw Group, the Borrowdale Volcanic Group, and the Windermere Supergroup. In addition there are a number of intrusive igneous rock masses, particularly in the north and west, which are exposed at the surface and also need to be considered (2.1, Table 2.1).

The Skiddaw Group

Rocks of the Skiddaw Group were known for many years as the Skiddaw Slates. Adam Sedgwick coined both terms in the early nineteenth century and it was the latter that came into common use. The former name recognises that not all Skiddaw rocks are slates – in fact after more than 180 years of research it's been concluded that true slates are not very common at all – and Skiddaw Group is now the official name, but many geologists refer to them simply as 'the Skiddaws'.

So, if they aren't all slates what are they? Sandstone, siltstone, mudstone, shale and breccia are the main rock types that make up the Skiddaw Group. They are all sedimentary rocks with evidence for metamorphism in certain areas and are up to 5000 m (yes, 5 km) in thickness. The Skiddaws are the oldest rocks exposed in the Lake District and were deposited during the early part of the Ordovician period (490–440 million years ago; Table 2.1) in deep water on the bed of the Iapetus Ocean. This ocean existed in high southern latitudes between the continents of Gondwana and Laurentia. The Skiddaws are not just old rocks they also are very far travelled.

Four areas of Skiddaw Group rocks are present in the Lake District (2.1); they are known as **inliers** because younger rocks surround them. In order of areal extent these are: the Skiddaw Inlier (480 km²), the Black Combe Inlier (50 km²), the Ullswater Inlier (22 km²) and the Bampton Inlier (12 km²). Only the first two of these form high ground. The Skiddaw Inlier extends from Mungrisdale in the east for about 40 km to Egremont in the west. It encompasses the summits and flanks of Blencathra, Skiddaw (2.3), the Lorton fells, the Grasmoor group, Robinson and Hindscarth, Maiden Moor and Cat Bells, the Loweswater fells, and several hills to the west of Ennerdale Water – Crag Fell, Grike, part of Lank Rigg and other smaller fells above Egremont. The Black Combe Inlier is centred on its namesake fell in the far southwest of the National Park; the Ullswater Inlier occupies low ground along much of the west shore of that lake and

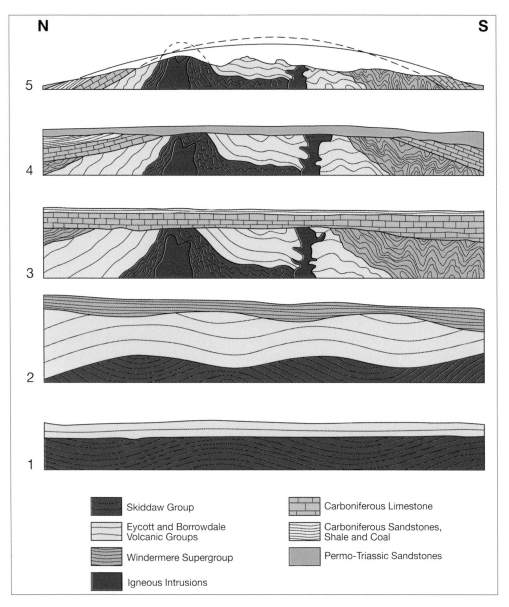

N   S

5

4

3

2

1

        Skiddaw Group   Carboniferous Limestone

        Eycott and Borrowdale   Carboniferous Sandstones,
        Volcanic Groups   Shale and Coal

        Windermere Supergroup   Permo-Triassic Sandstones

        Igneous Intrusions

2.2 Stages in the geological evolution of the Lake District. Stage 1, rocks of the Skiddaw Group have formed, they have been folded and eroded, and then buried by the Eycott and Borrowdale Volcanic Groups. Stage 2, the volcanic rocks have increased in thickness, as a result of more eruptions, they have been folded and eroded, and buried by rocks of the Windermere Supergroup. Stage 3, igneous masses have been intruded and the Caledonian Orogeny has caused uplift (mountain building) and folding. Erosion then occurred and the ancient mountain range was worn down and later covered by rocks of Carboniferous age. Stage 4, following uplift in the Hercynian Orogeny and erosion of the Carboniferous strata, sandstones of Permo-Triassic age were laid down. Stage 5, another phase of uplift was followed by erosion of the sandstones, and the dome-like structure of the Lake District with a core of older rocks surrounded by younger rocks had evolved. (British Geological Survey © NERC.)

2.3 Skiddaw Little Man and Lonscale Fell. Such relatively smooth steep slopes and rounded summits are often regarded as characteristic features of hills made from Skiddaw Group rocks.

the east shore north of Howtown, and the Bampton Inlier is a roughly north-south trending area to the east of Haweswater (2.1). Inliers of Skiddaw rocks also can be found on the eastern flanks of Cross Fell and in Teesdale in the Pennines, and rocks of similar age and type occur in the Isle of Man and southeast Ireland, although in these areas they are known by different names.

Skiddaw rocks are generally of dark colour – grey is the term most often used to describe them, with dark, medium or pale added where it has been thought appropriate. Blue, olive and greenish grey have also been applied to certain of the rock units in some areas. In general, the rocks are thinly bedded and laminated, and they have been contorted, folded and cleaved (2.4). As a result, where weathering has broken down the rocks, small, thin and flat fragments of scree are common (2.5). For this reason commercial working of these rocks was never likely to succeed.

Debate has raged for many years as to whether the Skiddaws were uplifted, folded and then eroded prior to formation of the overlying volcanic rocks. Most geologists now believe this to have been the case and it has been estimated that between 1000 m and 5000 m of rock is likely to have been removed by erosion. If the upper limit of that estimate is the correct value, then in some parts the Skiddaws are now less than half of their original thickness.

It has been said frequently that the Skiddaws are homogeneous and weak rocks, characteristics that have supposedly given rise to steep smooth slopes and rounded summits (2.3). This is not entirely true.

2.4 An example of folding in Skiddaw Group rocks in Mosedale (Caldew Valley). The scale bar divisions are 5 cm.

2.5 Skiddaw Group rocks usually breakdown into small flat fragments. The survey pole divisions are 20 cm.

2.6 Gasgale Crags, Whiteside, – rugged terrain on Skiddaw Group rocks.

Where sandstone beds are present or where the rocks have undergone some degree of metamorphic alteration, due to the proximity of igneous bodies, the terrain can be quite rugged, although not to the same extent as is found in the volcanic region of the central Lake District. Quite a number of Skiddaw fells display steep broken slopes – for example above Scales Tarn on Blencathra, Grasmoor End, and Gasgale Crags on Whiteside (2.6).

The Eycott and Borrowdale Volcanic Groups

The earliest volcanic rocks in the Lake District occur to the east of Mungrisdale, on Eycott Hill, and across a narrow area that includes High Pike, Brae Fell and Binsey to the north of the Skiddaw Inlier, and occupy about 50 km^2 of country (2.1). In the former area they are about 800 m thick, in the latter they attain a thickness in excess of 3000 m. They formed slightly earlier than the rocks of the Borrowdale Volcanic Group and are therefore regarded as a distinct group known as the Eycott Volcanic Group. Tabular sheets of basalt and andesite lavas (extrusive igneous rocks) are the dominant rock types. The eruptions that produced the lavas were mainly subaerial (land based) but because some inter-bedding with Skiddaw rocks occurs some eruptions were probably from submarine volcanic vents.

Green slate and porphyry is how Adam Sedgwick termed the rocks of the central Lake District. Today they are known as the Borrowdale Volcanic Group, or just as 'the Borrowdales'. Volcanic activity occurred during the middle part of the Ordovician period (490–440 million years ago; Table 2.1) and resulted in a great variety of extrusive rocks some of which testify to extremely violent eruptions. The Borrowdales are about 8000 m thick and extend north-south from near Keswick to the Duddon estuary and east-west from Shap to near Ravenglass, covering an area of 800 km^2 (2.1). The Scafells, Gable-Pillar, the Borrowdale fells, Coniston fells, Langdale fells, Helvellyn range, and High Street range are all made of the Borrowdale Volcanics (2.7 a and b).

The volcanic activity was associated with the gradual closing of the Iapetus Ocean as the continental plates drifted towards one another. These plate movements elevated the previously formed Skiddaw rocks and initiated a protracted period of subaerial volcanism. Present day eruptions along tectonic plate boundaries of the Pacific Rim are a modern analogue. Two phases of volcanic action are recognised in the Borrowdales. The first was characterised by effusive volcanism and was

2.7 Borrowdale Volcanic Group terrain: a, Broad Crag in the Scafell Pike range and b, Stybarrow Dodd in the Helvellyn range. The contrast could not be greater.

dominated by lava flows; explosive eruptions were infrequent. In the second phase explosive activity was the norm and resulted in a great variety of pyroclastic rocks.

Several types of lava are present and are distinguished on the basis of their silica content. Basalt is a basic (low silica) lava, dacite and rhyolite are acidic (high silica) lavas, and andesite is intermediate. These

2.8 Bedded tuffs (volcanic ash) exposed in the former quarry on Castle Crag in Borrowdale.

chemical variations are reflected in the colours of fresh rock surfaces with basic lavas being black or dark grey/blue and acid lavas pale grey. However, colour is only a guide to identification. On extrusion, low silica lavas are the most fluid, high silica lavas are much more viscous. As a consequence basalts can spread across large areas and create extensive sheets, whereas rhyolites tend to be of restricted extent and form thick dome-like masses.

The pyroclastic rocks have been sub-divided into pyroclastic fall, pyroclastic flow and pyroclastic surge deposits. They are composed of formerly molten or solidified materials that were fragmented by explosive eruptions and dispersed in air-borne plumes or as near surface clouds. Agglomerates and tuffs (volcanic ash) are fall-out deposits from plumes, and ignimbrites result from the flow of an incandescent mass of rock fragments and magma that weld together due to the high temperatures.

Fine-grained tuffs accumulated both on land (as air-fall tuffs) and in lakes (as volcaniclastic tuffs). Reworking of these materials by rivers and currents gave rise to water-lain bedded tuffs and these are distinctive and important members of the Borrowdales (2.8). They constitute Sedgwick's Green Slates and are found in two zones both of which trend southwest-northeast, one from Honister to Castle Crag and Grange Fell in Borrowdale, and the other from near Seathwaite in Dunnerdale to

2.9 Alternations of 'hard' lavas and 'soft' tuffs are responsible for the prominent stepping on the east side of High Rigg.

Coniston and Little and Great Langdale and on to Kirkstone, Kentmere and Longsleddale. For many years these tuffs have been worked for roofing and general building stone and ornamental pieces.

As with the Skiddaw rocks, the Borrowdales were folded and faulted and a great deal of material was removed by erosion prior to accumulation of the sediments of the overlying Windermere Supergroup.

In general terms, the volcanic rocks give rise to more rugged country than do the Skiddaws (2.7a), but they also underlie areas of rolling terrain (2.7b). This is because the Borrowdales consist of a great variety of rock types and, in spite of them sharing a common volcanic origin, they differ enormously with respect to their individual physical and chemical properties. The lavas are strong, physically resistant beds because they usually possess widely separated joints and fractures. As a consequence they stand out in the landscape as bold and precipitous rock faces. Some of the pyroclastic rocks are slightly less resistant due to a greater concentration of inherent weaknesses. An excellent example of this juxtaposition of 'hard' and 'soft' strata can be seen on the east side of High Rigg in St. John's in the Vale (2.9). Irrespective of these local variations, the physical breakdown of the Borrowdales results in blocks that are of considerably larger size than those deriving from the Skiddaws (2.10).

2.10 Borrowdale Volcanic Group rocks usually breakdown into blocks that are considerably larger than those from the Skiddaw Group (compare with 2.5). The survey pole divisions are 20 cm.

The Windermere Supergroup

Cessation of Borrowdale volcanicity and erosion of the rocks was followed by subsidence of the landmass and marine condition became dominant once again. From the late Ordovician to the end of the Silurian period (440–415 million years ago; Table 2.1) enormous quantities of sediment accumulated as the Iapetus Ocean deepened and closed. Some 8000 m of mudstone, siltstone, sandstone, gritstone and limestone was formed and now occupies most of the Lake District south of a line running from the Duddon estuary to Coniston, Ambleside and on to between Shap and Tebay (2.1). These rocks also extend well beyond the boundary of the National Park covering the area between Kendal, Tebay, Sedbergh, Dent and Kirkby Lonsdale, including the Howgill Fells.

Within the Lake District, Windermere rocks underlie fell country that is of lower relief and thus less dramatic than that associated with the Skiddaws and Borrowdales. The terrain is more subdued and has a gentler aspect than that to its north (2.11). Nevertheless there are variations in hardness between the different strata that give rise to distinctive patterns in the landscape. Harder rock types stand out as prominent elevations with crags, softer rocks have undergone greater denudation and are sites of valleys and depressions (2.12). Overall a topography of ridges and vales has developed and can be best appreciated by walking or driving around Grizedale Forest between Coniston Water and Windermere (assuming

2.11 Windermere Supergroup rocks underlie terrain that is of lower relief and considerably less dramatic than that associated with the Skiddaw and Borrowdale rocks.

2.12 Where the Windermere Supergroup rocks crop out they usually give rise to low broken crags.

the trees don't obscure your view), or by simply studying the contours of the OS map. The higher ground itself is frequently a mosaic of rocky knolls and wet, peaty hollows. What the terrain lacks in scale it makes up for in complexity.

Intrusive igneous rocks

A number of igneous intrusions occur in the Lake District but the individual areas of outcrop are very small in comparison to the rock groups considered previously (2.1, Table 2.1). Most of the intrusions are of acidic composition, such as granite and granophyre, but there are also basic rocks, such as dolerite and gabbro. The intrusions are thought to be connected deep below the surface and to represent parts of a huge composite batholith that continues below the Irish Sea and Isle of Man to the west and below the Pennines to the east. Segments of the batholith were intruded at different times. The intrusions are significant with respect to both geomorphology and industry. In the first instance marked variations in the local landscape occur because of differences in rock character and because there has been some degree of metamorphism of the country rock. In the second, some intrusions have been exploited as sources of construction stone, and in times past their associated mineral veins yielded valuable ores.

The earliest intrusive phase was contemporary with the Eycott Volcanic Group and resulted in emplacement of the **Carrock Fell Complex.** The outcrop extends along the northern side of Mosedale, from the hamlet of that name to the head of Roughten Gill. Gabbro, diabase and granophyre are the main rock types and can be seen in the crags and fallen boulders along the low east end of Carrock Fell and in the area between the summit ridge and the steep drop into Mosedale. Different components of the complex were emplaced at different times: the gabbro about 470 million years ago, the diabase shortly afterwards, and the granophyre about 420 million years ago.

At three valley locations north of Blencathra there are outcrops of the **Skiddaw Granite**. This is a white to grey granite and can be seen around the confluence of Grainsgill Beck and the River Caldew, between the confluences of the Caldew with Blackhazel Beck and Wiley Gill, and in Sinen Gill. The granite was intruded about 400 million years ago. Together the Skiddaw Granite and Carrock Fell Complex have resulted in the metamorphism of the adjacent Skiddaw Group rocks and more recent erosion has emphasised this alteration through the creation of prominent crags above Bowscale Tarn and on the north side of Mosedale.

On either side of the northern end of St. John's in the Vale is the outcrop of the **Threlkeld Microgranite**. This is a grey fine-grained rock intruded between the Skiddaw and Borrowdale groups but with little evidence of having achieved any significant metamorphic alteration. The eastern outcrop, which has been extensively quarried, underlies the distinctive knobbly summit of Threlkeld Knotts directly below the Red Screes face of Clough Head. The western outcrop underlies Low Rigg and Tewet Tarn. An age of 445 million years has been determined for the intrusion.

Probably the most distinctive of the Lake District intrusive rocks is the **Shap Granite**, which was emplaced about 393 million years ago along the boundary of the Borrowdale and Windermere rocks, both of which were metamorphosed. The granite is coarse-grained and contains large elongated crystals of pink feldspar that give it an attractiveness and value as polished ornamental stone. Because it is easily recognised, Shap Granite **erratics** in glacial sediments have been used to infer patterns and directions of ice movement during the last glaciation of northern England.

The **Eskdale Intrusion (granite and granodiorite)** represents the largest exposure of the Lake District granitic batholith. There are two outcrops: the smaller occurs at Wasdale Head, the larger underlies much of middle and lower Eskdale, the whole of Miterdale and the valley of Whillan Beck, and the coastal foothills extending south to the vicinity of Bootle. Granite is found to the north and east of Muncaster Fell with granodiorite to the south. The intrusion invaded the Borrowdale rocks about 450 million years ago.

On either side of Ennerdale Water and extending south to the foot of Wast Water and north to Buttermere is the three-part outcrop of the **Ennerdale Granite**. The intrusion was emplaced into the Skiddaw and Borrowdale rocks about 452 million years ago. The distinctive pink rock is particularly conspicuous on the eroded path that rises from Bleaberry Tarn to Red Pike above Buttermere.

Numerous other minor intrusions are found throughout the Lake District but to describe them all is beyond the scope of this book. Suffice to say that many are sills and dykes of basalt and dolerite up to a few tens of metres in thickness. Because many have proved to be less resistant to weathering than the host rocks they intruded they have acted as sites for cols on ridges and gully development on hillsides. Two of the most spectacular examples are Mickledore, between Scafell Pike and Scafell, and Lord's Rake that slants across the crags of the latter mountain.

Mountain building and younger rocks

The period of geological history from the early Ordovician to the end of the Silurian in which most of the rocks described above were created was very important for the Lake District in another respect. At various times uplift and erosion of the rocks had occurred but the major phase of mountain building – the **Caledonian Orogeny** – took place at the end of the Silurian period and beginning of the Devonian, around 420–400 million years ago (2.2, Table 2.1). The remains of the Iapetus Ocean were finally destroyed as the continents collided and welded together to form a new landmass, and along the junction a mountain chain was thrust up. Uplift was not restricted to the Lake District; rocks in the Highlands of Scotland, Scandinavia, eastern Greenland and northeastern North America were also affected and all these areas are said to possess a Caledonian trend.

Mountain building resulted in deformation of the rocks, and folds aligned southwest – northeast developed. The Skiddaw rocks and weaker strata of the Windermere rocks underwent the most complex folding; the Borrowdale rocks and stronger strata of the Windermere rocks display broader folds or, in some cases, none at all. Fracturing and faulting were associated with the folding and some Lake District valleys follow such lines of weakness because processes of denudation have found these zones easier to exploit.

An enormous amount of geological time – some 400 million years – has passed since the Caledonian Orogeny and although various types of rock have been created subsequently, they are not particularly common within the Lake District. A zone of Devonian (415–360 million years ago) conglomerate extends from Great Mell Fell to Pooley Bridge at the northern end of Ullswater and for 3 km along the valley of the River Eamont. Carboniferous (360–300 million years ago) limestones occur around Caldbeck, between Askham and Shap in the Lowther valley, and form the prominent 'scars' of Cunswick, Scout and Whitbarrow to the west and southwest of Kendal (2.1). Later in the Carboniferous, sandstones, shales and coals were formed and are found beyond the boundary of the National Park in a broad area between Maryport and Whitehaven.

At the end of the Carboniferous another phase of uplift – the **Hercynian Orogeny** – affected the Lake District (2.2, Table 2.1). This period of mountain building was less severe than the earlier one but the rocks were raised into a gentle dome. Erosion then removed the

Carboniferous strata from over the centre of the dome leaving them as a rim surrounding the core of older rocks.

Along the coast, from St. Bees Head to Millom, on the Solway plain, and in the Vale of Eden, to the east of the Lake District, New Red Sandstones of Permo-Triassic age (300–200 million years ago) are found (2.1). The coastal outcrop is partly within the National Park and these are the youngest rocks in the Lake District. It is thought that the sandstones previously covered the older rocks and, like the Carboniferous rocks, they were stripped away by erosion.

There are no rocks of Jurassic, Cretaceous or Tertiary age in the Lake District and little evidence for them having ever existed. However, rocks from these periods are well represented in other parts of Great Britain and some geologists believe that their absence from the National Park is not because they never formed but because they too have been removed by erosion. If that is so, then the erosion didn't leave even a rim of these rocks around the central core, except perhaps for an area of Jurassic strata to the west of Carlisle.

Irrespective of whether any rocks formed in the Lake District during the Tertiary (65–2.6 million years ago) it is an important period with respect to the development of mountain landforms for it has long been considered that this was the interval in which the drainage pattern developed. Of greater importance is the Quaternary (the last 2.6 million years) because most of the landforms described and explained in Chapters 4–8 result from processes of erosion and deposition associated with the marked changes in climate that are known to have occurred over that time (Table 2.1). Indeed, some of those same processes operate at the present day and therefore landform modification and creation continues. Present day processes and changes may seem rather insignificant and small when compared to what has happened in the past but they demonstrate that the landscape is dynamic and will remain so. Our ability to see and appreciate the bigger picture of geomorphological change is often limited by the rather short time we inhabit the Earth. It is by using examples from mountain ranges in other environments that we can begin to construct a model of how, why and when the Lake District landforms evolved.

CHAPTER THREE

The pre-glacial landscape

Introduction

- What did the Lake District look like prior to glaciation?
- Does the Lake District retain vestiges of that pre-glacial landscape?
- If so, where are those landscape remnants and what distinctive characteristics do they possess?
- How certain can we be that these areas were not greatly modified by ice erosion?

THESE QUESTIONS HAVE EXERCISED the minds of geologists and geomorphologists for a long time because they are pertinent with respect to what happened or might have happened during the 60 million years or so of the Tertiary period, which was briefly mentioned at the end of the Chapter 2, and during the Quaternary period, spanning the last 2.6 million years.

It has often been said that the Lake District displays all the signs of vigorous erosion by former glaciers. While this may be true it does not necessarily mean that all the evidence for the pre-glacial landscape has been obliterated. Ever since the glacial theory gained wide acceptance in the mid-nineteenth century the issue of whether an earlier landscape, or parts of it, could be recognised has been debated in the scientific literature. But it is not just in the Lake District that evidence for pre-glacial topography has been sought; similar studies have focussed on other upland areas of Great Britain – Wales and the Highlands of Scotland in particular – and it has also been argued that parts of the Scandinavian pre-glacial landscape survived unscathed in spite of the passage of enormous ice-sheets and glaciers.

Lately, this topic has received much less attention from geomorpholo-

THE PRE-GLACIAL LANDSCAPE   • 33 •

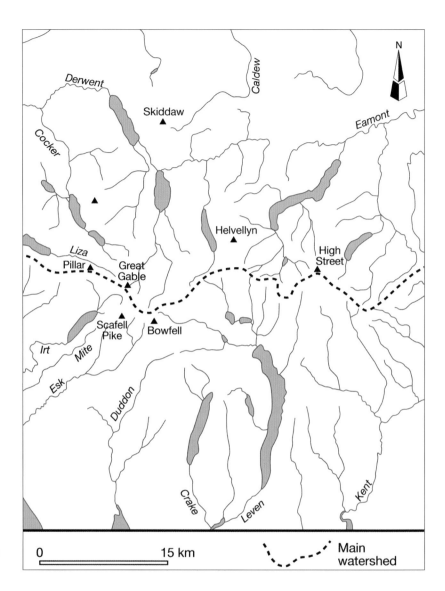

3.1 The drainage pattern of the Lake District.

gists than it did previously. Nevertheless, if the existing topographical variations and evolution of the Lake District landscape are to be explained it is still a very relevant subject, although one that is rather difficult to evaluate.

In this chapter some of the inherited components of the landscape as proposed and discussed by many people over many years are described. It needs to be said that not all geomorphologists accept this 'survival thesis', some believing that the physical landscape of the Lake District is, in its entirety, a product of repeated glaciation. The chapter has not

LAKE DISTRICT MOUNTAIN LANDFORMS

been written so as to reflect my own
views on this subject and it is not my
intention to draw firm conclusions
about the matter. Rather, it presents
the 'evidence', as others before me
have. It is left to you to assess the
validity of this and form your own
opinions.

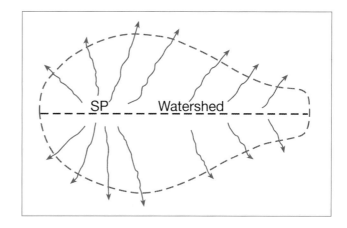

The drainage pattern

In his *Guide to the Lakes* William Wordsworth likened the drainage
pattern to one that is 'diverging.....like spokes from the nave of a wheel'.
He had recognised that many, but not all, of the valleys radiated from close
to a common area around Great Gable and Scafell. Seven major valleys
begin near there: Langdale, Dunnerdale, Eskdale, Wasdale, Ennerdale,
Buttermere-Crummock, and Borrowdale (3.1). But several other major
valleys, principally those in the eastern part of the Lake District, do not
start near Wordsworth's 'nave' and therefore they do not fit with the
notion of a radial drainage pattern.

The Cambridge professor, John Marr considered the drainage system
to be like one that would develop on the surface of an up-turned caddy
spoon (3.2). Drainage from the inverted 'bowl' of the spoon (near Scafell
Pike) would be radial and that from the 'handle' (east of the Helvellyn
range) would be oblique to the roughly west-east aligned watershed. This
pattern is probably the simplest way of representing and describing the
system. Unfortunately the misleading term 'radial' is still used in some
texts that describe the Lake District landscape.

How and when the drainage pattern developed is another issue that
has been debated at some length. It is widely acknowledged that the
pattern originated prior to the Quaternary period of geological time, but
just when valley incision began is not known.

One of the problems facing geomorphologists when attempting to
explain the drainage pattern is why the major rivers adopt the arrangement
they do rather than following the basic west-southwest to east-northeast
structural grain of the main rock groups. After all, rivers tend to erode their
valleys along lines of least resistance in the bedrock, which are frequently
aligned parallel with the grain. In the Lake District many rivers and valleys
cut across the structural grain and therefore are said to exhibit discordance.

3.2 The caddy spoon
drainage pattern as
proposed by Professor
John Marr. SP
represents Scafell Pike.

Discordant drainage patterns are usually explained in terms of the superimposition of drainage from a cover of younger rocks that has now disappeared. Accordingly, as the Lake District rivers cut down through the younger rocks they eventually came into contact with the underlying and older rock groups (the Windermeres, Borrowdales and Skiddaws) and continued to flow across these strata along their established directions. Eventually erosion removed all traces of the younger rocks, leaving an arrangement of superimposed rivers. For over 100 years this interpretation of the Lake District drainage pattern has held sway.

However, there are difficulties with this explanation. It cannot be demonstrated conclusively that the rivers were superimposed from a cover of younger rocks because those rocks do not occur anywhere in the central Lake District at the present day. The rock cover on which the drainage pattern was supposedly initiated is said to have comprised either the New Red Sandstone, which today occurs around the margins of the area, or Chalk of Cretaceous age, which is not found around the margins. If the drainage system was initiated on the former rocks, it has had about 200 million years in which to develop but only 65 million years if initiated on the latter rocks. Speculation and assumption have formed part of the hypothesis but that does not necessarily mean it should be rejected.

So, if superimposition cannot satisfactorily explain the drainage pattern, what can?

The Lake District rocks are traversed by numerous faults and fractures, many of which result from earth movements during the Caledonian Orogeny. Some of these are parallel to the structural grain but others cut across it. Detailed geological mapping, using aerial photographs, satellite images and groundtruthing (aka serious legwork!), has shown that many valleys have developed along these zones of weakness. One major fault (the Coniston Fault) runs north from Coniston via Red Bank, Grasmere, Dunmail Raise, Thirlmere, and St. John's in the Vale to Threlkeld (3.3). Parts of Great Langdale, Eskdale, Wasdale, Ullswater and Windermere, to name just a few, also follow fault or fracture lines. But faulting and fracturing cannot account for all valley alignments; Ennerdale, Newlands and parts of upper Eskdale and upper Borrowdale are examples that are not fault- or fracture-related. In the mid-nineteenth century faulting was thought to have been an important control on valley development; around the end of the century it had been discounted and replaced by the superimposition theory; now faulting is back in favour!

Writing in the 1950s, Professor David Linton considered that vigorous glacial erosion during the Quaternary had had a significant

influence on valley locations and alignments in upland regions. In essence
he regarded past episodes of glaciation as capable of either modifying or
initiating systems of valleys. He thought that the Lake District's original
drainage pattern had extended north and south from a west-east watershed rather than having a radial component to it. The repeated build up
of an ice-dome during the Quaternary and its associated outward-flowing
ice-streams was regarded as a mechanism capable of transforming that
pattern into one with a distinct radial element to it in the western part of
the area. That glaciers can modify the landscape is not in doubt; whether
the present drainage pattern was created by glaciation or merely served to
guide ice flow along pre-existing routes is much less certain.

There is the possibility that the present drainage pattern results from
some combination of the mechanisms outlined above. It is does not have
to have been created by a single one. We simply do not know and may
never know how and when the pattern was initiated.

Other aspects of the drainage system arising from glaciation and also
from post-glacial river activity are considered in Chapters 4 and 7.

Subdued terrain

Subdued terrain comprises smooth, gently sloping or flattened hillcrests,
rounded slopes of moderate gradient relative to those lower on the valley
sides, areas of gently undulating or rolling landscape and broad open valley

3.4 Subdued terrain (the 'elevated downs' of Thomas Hay) is much in evidence on the ridge of the Dodds.

heads. Thomas Hay referred to such areas as 'elevated downs'. They have an almost unbroken cover of soil and vegetation with very few protruding outcrops of rock and have been recognised in several parts of the Lake District. It has been considered that they represent either unmodified or only slightly modified fragments of the pre-glacial landscape.

The upper parts of many fells possess features characteristic of subdued terrain: the main areas are the hills at the Back o'Skiddaw, the Helvellyn ridge and the Dodds to its north (3.4), the northern part of the High Street ridge, the area east and northeast of Longsleddale, and several of the fells located close to the western margin of the Lake District. Even the summit areas of Pillar, Great Gable, and Grasmoor have been thought of as remnants of the subdued terrain.

Differences in the local geology might be considered to account for these scenic contrasts but in most cases this is unlikely to be the cause. Compare the eastern face of the ridge between Dollywaggon Pike and Helvellyn, with its deep rough coves and cliffed headwalls, and the west-facing slopes of the same ridge, with their long and smooth convex profiles above about 600 m (3.5). The rock types are essentially the same on both sides of the ridge but the contrast in topography couldn't be greater and is a reflection of the variation in the intensity of glacial erosion – severe on the east, considerably less severe on the west.

Another area of great scenic contrast, although less well known than the Helvellyn ridge, is the valley of Mosedale-Swindale in the east of the Lake District. The head of Mosedale is on the eastern side of the broad col between Tarn Crag and Branstree, at about 500 m. For 3–4 km downstream, the river occupies a wide, gradually descending valley with gently- to moderately-sloping sides. Then at a height of about 400 m the river drops 120 m in 500 m, via falls and cascades, to Swindale with its characteristic glacial valley profile of flat floor and steep cliff-girt sides. It is as if the glaciers gave Mosedale just a 'light touch' allowing it to retain much of its pre-glacial form.

Profiles across Lake District valleys often reveal valley-in-valley forms (3.6). These can be 'seen' from a study of map contours as well as by walking the ground. The northern flanks of Mosedale at the Back

3.5 A number of rough coves bite deeply into the eastern side of the Helvellyn ridge. In contrast the western and south-western slopes are considerably smoother as shown by the flanks of Dollywaggon Pike directly behind the walker.

3.6 Sketch of the cross-sectional valley-in-valley form of some Lake District valleys.

3.7 The valley-in-valley form is seen here on Sheffield Pike. The upper slopes of the fell descend at a moderate gradient as far as the top of the crags where the gradient suddenly increases.

pre-glacial valley profile

glaciated valley

o'Skiddaw are a clear example. If you walk south from the summit of Carrock Fell you descend at a moderate gradient for about 1 km. At a height of about 450 m the gradient suddenly increases and the hillside falls for 200 m in less than 400 m to the valley floor. The upper slopes may be remnants of the valley sides that existed prior to glaciation. If that is so then the valley was previously higher and broader and over successive glacial phases has been deepened by over 200 m. Another good example can be seen on the southern slopes of Sheffield Pike above Glenridding where there is a marked change in gradient around the 550 m contour (3.7).

Most, if not all, of the subdued terrain would have had a cover of glacier ice at some stage during the Quaternary period as shown by the presence there of thin layers of glacial sediment and scattered **erratic** boulders. Therefore, we may think of these areas as having undergone relatively minor amounts of modification by the ice-sheets. It has been said that away from the coves and the trough-like valleys the landscape is much as it was before the very first phase of glacial activity.

Erosion surfaces

Erosion surfaces (sometimes called planation surfaces) are low gradient land surfaces that cut indiscriminately across underlying geological structures. They result from lengthy periods of erosion and, if formed at different altitudes, create a stepped or tiered topography of low relative relief. Therefore an overlap exists between erosion surfaces and the subdued terrain described earlier. Often the subdued terrain occurs within altitude zones that correspond to putative erosion surfaces.

In the Lake District, erosion surfaces have been identified at several altitudes and because glacial valleys dissect them and some have a cover of glacial sediment and erratic boulders, they are regarded as pre-glacial although their exact ages are unclear. The existing erosion surfaces are thought to be remnants of more extensive surfaces that would have been very distinctive features of the pre-glacial landscape.

The recognition of erosion surfaces in the Lake District has been based on the examination of topographic maps and on field surveys. To the non-specialist it may not at first be apparent that remnants of erosion surfaces can be seen in the Lake District and there are some geomorphologists who are sceptical about the survival of such landforms, if indeed they were ever present. However from many elevated vantage points, views across

3.8 Some geomorph-
ologists would recognise
two or three erosion
surface levels in this view
across Kirk Fell and the
Pillar range.

Lakeland are of summit plateaus, gently-sloping ridges, bevelled spurs and flattened shoulders, and steps or ramps leading from one level to another (3.8). These features have been documented at several altitudes across most of the Lake District height range.

Surfaces that fall within the same narrow height range have been thought of as being contemporaneous features – they were eroded at the same time. For example, there are quite a few plateau-like summits within the 762–808 m height range in the Coniston fells and the High Street range, similarly a large number of summit elevations cluster around 300 m in the area underlain by the Windermere rocks. In both cases these have been regarded as remnants of formerly more widespread surfaces.

How such surfaces at accordant altitudes were created is a contentious issue. They have been attributed to subaerial erosion and to marine erosion. Some geomorphologists favour a marine origin for all the surfaces, with the highest surface being the first to be cut at a time of stationary sea level. As sea level fell and then stabilised the next highest surface was created, and so on. Thus, the surfaces represent a relative age sequence from highest (oldest) to lowest (youngest). An alternative hypothesis states that the higher surfaces stem from subaerial erosion and the lower ones from progressive falls in sea level. If that were so, the relative ages of the surfaces in each category would follow the same pattern as before. Of course, it could be much more complex than that. Once again, we simply do not know.

3.9 Diagram indicating
how the morphology
of erosion surfaces has
been modified by glacial
erosion.

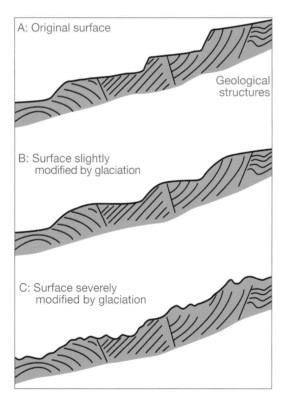

A: Original surface

Geological
structures

B: Surface slightly
modified by glaciation

C: Surface severely
modified by glaciation

3.10 a, The Fairfield Horseshoe ridge corresponds to part B of 3.9 – it rises (or falls) in a series of smooth steps; b, The ridge from Loughrigg Fell to Blea Rigg is of similar form to part C of 3.9 – it rises (or falls) in a series of rugged steps. The picture shows the Dow Bank to Silver How section of the ridge.

The three cross-sections shown in 3.9 are designed to illustrate the original and present-day morphology of erosion surfaces. Part **A** shows an irregular staircase-like sequence of surfaces resulting from either subaerial or marine erosion. Surfaces are gently sloping and are separated by steps of substantially steeper gradient. In **B**, the surfaces have been slightly modified by glacial erosion but the stepped sequence is still very obvious. The ridge that leads from Nab Scar via Heron Pike and Greatrigg Man to Fairfield is of this type (3.10a). In **C**, the surfaces have been severely modified by glacial action; the terrain is much more irregular but surface remnants and the position of steps can still be identified. The ridge from Loughrigg Fell via Silver How and Castle How to Blea Rigg has this form (3.10b).

Summary

It is difficult to provide wholly convincing explanations for the origins of the landforms described in this chapter and what the landscape looked like before glaciation is virtually impossible to know. Nevertheless, if we did know the landscape character prior to glaciation then we would be in a much better position to assess the effectiveness of glacial erosion. The types of study that identified subdued terrain and erosion surfaces have been neglected for some time now; there is a need for a more modern approach using more sophisticated techniques of analysis in order to answer some long-standing questions.

CHAPTER FOUR

Glaciation and related landforms

Introduction

THE LAKE DISTRICT LANDSCAPE IS one that shows the very clear impacts of glaciation. Glaciation is not only responsible for having carved out some extremely distinctive features, it has also left a legacy of widespread deposits with conspicuous surface form. These landforms of erosion and deposition have been subjected to detailed study with a view to understanding and explaining their relationship to glacier development and decay. However, geomorphologists are still debating the age and origin of some of these features.

Prior to 1840 geologists regarded the superficial deposits that cover much of Great Britain as being of diluvial origin – that is, they were seen as products of a great deluge that was equated with the Biblical Flood. The Reverend William Buckland, Professor of Mineralogy and Geology at Oxford, was a prominent advocate of diluvialism and wrote extensively about it. But following a visit to the Alps in 1838 and a tour of northern England and Scotland in 1840 with the Swiss geologist Louis Agassiz, Buckland was converted to the **Glacial Theory** that Agassiz and others had proposed to explain certain landforms in the greater alpine region. From this time on most of the superficial deposits of Great Britain began to be interpreted as being of glacial origin

Not all geologists were as enthusiastic as Agassiz and Buckland about former land-based glaciation. For some years a compromise (diluvial-glacial) view, in which the glaciers were thought to have comprised floating ice masses, prevailed. Writing in the 1870s, Clifton Ward discussed the previous existence of floating ice in the Lake District and how this could account for various features. In the latter part of the nineteenth century the diluvial component of this modified theory was gradually abandoned and prominence was given once more to land-based ice.

The glaciations that shaped the Lake District occurred during the Quaternary period and possibly in the latter part of the preceding Tertiary period. Much earlier phases of glaciation have also occurred in the Earth's history and the evidence for these is contained within the **rock record**. Several of these phases were in the Pre-Cambrian period – long before any of the Lake District rocks were created – other glaciations occurred in the Ordovician, Devonian and Permo-Carboniferous periods but the areas they affected were far away from the evolving 'Lake District'.

The global cooling of climate that culminated in widespread and repeated Quaternary glaciations began during the Tertiary period. The Antarctic ice-sheets may have developed 30–40 million years ago while in the northern hemisphere the first glaciers probably formed around 10–15 million years ago in Arctic latitudes. Since those times, glaciers have waxed and waned as global climate has fluctuated – phases of glaciation have alternated with phases without glaciers, when climate was as warm as, or warmer than, that at present. These warmer interludes are known as **interglacials**. Even though glacier ice still occurs on certain parts of the Earth, the planet has been in interglacial mode for the last 11,500 years.

Currently the bulk of glacier ice is to be found in Antarctica (86%) and Greenland (11%). The remaining 3% occurs on Arctic islands and on high mountains. Glaciers occupy about 10% of the Earth's land surface; in past glacial phases at least 30% of the land was ice covered – including the Lake District.

Just how many times glaciers developed in the Lake District is a very difficult question to answer. Trying to determine the number of glaciations anywhere has been likened to counting the number of times a whiteboard has been wiped clean. Each glaciation has had the annoying habit of destroying much of the evidence left by its predecessor, and it has proved extremely difficult to work back and produce a reliable estimate.

One indication for the number times that glaciers have existed in the Lake District (and for that matter in the mid-to-high latitudes of the northern hemisphere in general) is contained in sediments that have built up on the floor of the deep oceans. Although the accumulation rate of oceanic sediment is low, it has been more or less continuous and disturbance has been negligible. In some places these sediments extend back several millions of years. As global climate shifted from warm to cold and back to warm the marine micro-organisms also changed. Analysis of fossil micro-organisms in sediment cores has enabled scientists to conclude that there have probably been in the region of 50 episodes of Quaternary glaciation.

This does not necessarily mean that the Lake District has been glaciated 50 times. The deep ocean sediments do not tell us the exact locations and extents of the glaciers and ice-sheets. Furthermore the glacial intervals were not all the same length, nor were they of equal severity. It is likely that Great Britain escaped glaciation at certain times even though an extremely cold climate prevailed. On some occasions glaciation was probably short-lived and restricted to upland areas like the Lake District; on other occasions all of the country to as far south as a line running from London to Bristol and along the north coast of the southwest peninsula was inundated.

We know from the deposits that exist in the Threlkeld area that there have been at least three episodes of Lake District glaciation. This is considerably less than the 50 episodes that might have occurred according to the ocean sediments. The exact number of times that glaciers developed in the Lake District may never be known but it is probably fair to assume it is somewhat more than three.

To help us understand how the Lake District looked during glacial phases we can examine glaciers and ice-sheets in other parts of the world. This approach can provide us with some important clues and along with the recognition of glacial landforms we can begin to construct a picture of the Lake District under different amounts and extents of ice.

During some glaciations the entire Lake District was probably buried beneath its own ice-sheet that coalesced around its margins with ice moving south from Scotland and ice generated in the northern Pennines. Erratic rocks from Scotland have never been found in the Lake District mountains although they do occur in the surrounding lowlands. This has been taken as an indication that Lake District ice was powerful enough to deflect Scottish ice and prevent it from invading the area. These would have been the occasions when ice extended south to the English Midlands and beyond.

At other times glaciation was more restricted and ice was limited to the high coves, the upper reaches of some valleys, and to adjacent mountain summits. These conditions would have existed during the build up and subsequent decay of the Lake District ice-sheet but they also occurred as distinct episodes of glaciation – that is to say, on some occasions expansion and merging of these relatively small glaciers to create an ice-sheet did not happen. 4.1 and 4.2 showing present day glaciers in Baffin Island and the Austrian Alps give some indications of how the Lake District may have looked at different stages of glaciation.

Of the three glacial episodes known to have affected the Lake District

4.1 This picture of Baffin Island is probably a reasonable representation of how the Lake District looked about 20,000 years ago as the Late Devensian ice-sheet began to wane.

the earliest of these probably occurred between 300,000 and 500,000 years ago. The deposits of this glaciation are deeply weathered suggesting that they needed long periods of temperate conditions (interglacials) to acquire this characteristic. They are also buried beneath the deposits of more recent glaciation.

The other two episodes occurred during the **Devensian** cold stage that began about 115,000 years ago following the **Ipswichian** interglacial. The Devensian was a long cold period that was interrupted on several occasions by less cold interludes each lasting up to a few thousands of years. The ocean sediments indicate that glaciers existed in much of northern Europe during the early and middle Devensian but in the Lake District the situation is thought to have been one of restricted glaciation.

Around 30,000–25,000 years ago a substantial expansion of the mountain glaciers took place and this culminated about 21,000 years ago in an ice-sheet that covered most, if not all, of Scotland, Wales and

LAKE DISTRICT MOUNTAIN LANDFORMS

northern England. The Midlands and southern England lay beyond the ice margin. Evidence from the western part of the Lake District suggests complete ice coverage at this time although some summits above approximately 850 m, including Bowfell, Great Gable, Pillar and those of the Scafell Pike range, may have protruded above the ice-sheet as **nunataks**. Eventually this **Late Devensian** ice-sheet began to wane and by about 15,000 years ago the ice had probably gone completely from the Lake District.

For the next 2,000 years or so a more temperate climate occurred and the landscape was colonised by a variety of plants including juniper and birch. However, 13,000 years ago there was an abrupt cooling of climate and glaciers once more began to develop in the Lake District mountains. This was a restricted and short-lived glaciation; the glaciers had gone from the coves, valley head and plateau areas by 11,500 years ago. This final period of glaciation is known as the **Loch Lomond Glaciation** because it was in the Loch Lomond area of Scotland that, in the latter part of the

4.2 The lower section of a decaying valley glacier in Austria – a situation that existed across Lakeland about 18,000 years ago.

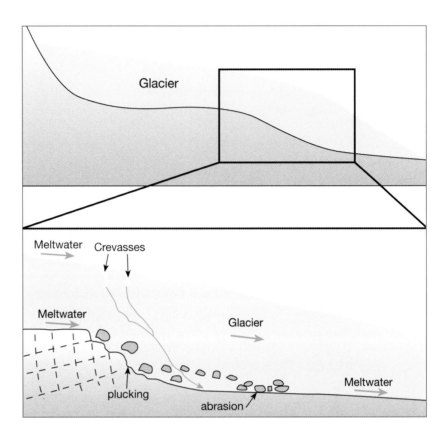

4.3 Schematic long-section through a glacier showing meltwater movement and areas of plucking and abrasion.

nineteenth century, geomorphological evidence for this glacial phase was first recognised.

With the warming of climate that caused these glaciers to disappear from the Lake District came the gradual colonisation of the landscape by deciduous woodland and by humans. However, this **post-glacial** period has not been one of uninterrupted warmth; there have been several occasions, from decades to centuries in length, when climate has taken a turn for the worse. But the severe conditions required to nourish mountain glaciers have not returned.

It was estimated by Professor Gordon Manley that under present climatic conditions the highest summits of the Lake District would require about another 800–900 m of elevation in order to have permanent snowfields. With the present trend towards increasing warmth we are unlikely to see the snowline falling and glaciers returning to the Lake District in the near future. Nevertheless we have an abundance of landforms that demonstrate the effects of past glaciation and it is these that contribute in large measure to the diversity of landscape.

Glacial erosion

Landforms of glacial erosion develop because ice moving across the land surface is capable of removing, picking up, and transporting bedrock and sediment. Removal of material takes place as a result of **plucking** (aka quarrying), **abrasion**, and **glacial meltwater erosion** (4.3). These processes of erosion have been observed below and at the margins of modern glaciers and ice-sheets, and because some Lake District landforms bear a striking resemblance to those emerging from beneath retreating glaciers in the Alps and Scandinavia it is inferred that they were produced by similar processes.

Plucking refers to the crushing or fracturing of rock beneath the ice and the entrainment of the broken rock into the ice. By this means different sized lumps of rock are removed and carried away (4.4a). **Abrasion** occurs when particles of rock that have been incorporated into the ice by plucking come into contact with one another or with the underlying bedrock. The process has been likened to sandpapering and the effect is a progressive wearing down of the rock surfaces with smoothing and/or polishing being evident (4.4b). Both mechanical and chemical processes are involved in erosion by **meltwater** flowing alongside, beneath and away from glaciers. The ability of meltwater to erode is related to the character of the bedrock, the velocity of the water, and the amount of sediment being carried by the flow.

4.4 a, Plucked surface of Borrowdale Volcanic Group rock above Stockley Bridge, the survey pole divisions are 20 cm; b, An abraded and polished surface of Skiddaw Group rock at Grange, the scale bar divisions are 5 cm.

The amount and nature of erosion achieved by any particular glacier is also linked to the thermal properties at the base of the ice. A **warm-based** glacier has meltwater at its base, which helps the glacier to slide along and erode (4.3). A **cold-based** glacier does not slide and the amount of erosion tends to be limited. A **warm-based** glacier may seem to be a contradiction in terms but temperature at the base of a glacier is a function of the ice thickness, frictional heat, and geothermal heat. **Warm-based** glaciers accomplish more erosion than **cold-based** ones because they are relatively fast-moving ice masses. Over time the thermal properties of glaciers can change and as a consequence erosion rates will also change. It becomes extremely difficult to say exactly how long it has taken for any particular landform of glacial erosion to attain its morphology.

It has to be remembered that we don't know in detail how the landscape looked before the start of the first glaciation, as was explained in Chapter 3, and therefore we can't be certain how much erosion was achieved by successive ice advances. We also don't know how many advances there have been. Whilst it is probably true that the larger landforms have been fashioned by repeated glaciation, some of the smaller ones were most likely created during one or other of the last two glacial episodes between 25,000 and 11,500 years ago.

Before describing the most commonly encountered landforms of glacial erosion in the Lake District another thing need to be said. These landforms range in scale from large to small and the small-scale forms are often found superimposed on intermediate-scale forms, and the latter are components of larger-scale features. Whilst we readily place landforms in such categories we should not forget that they share a common heritage and together create distinctive landscapes.

Landforms of glacial erosion

Glaciated Valleys

Glaciated valleys are probably the most obvious landforms resulting from erosion by glaciers in the Lake District (4.5). Although frequently referred to as 'U-shaped' valleys, very few have a true U-shape in cross-section and a more appropriate descriptive term is **glacial troughs**. This term recognises that the valleys are linear features that have been eroded deeply into the bedrock and, because most troughs are asymmetric, it also allows for inclusion of different cross-sectional forms (4.6). To understand why the

4.5 The Buttermere valley – a classical glacial trough.

cross-sectional shape of troughs can differ or why an individual trough changes shape along its course we need to know about local variations in rock types and their properties, such as strength and joint spacing. Deep narrow troughs are usually associated with areas of high rock strength.

In all probability the Lake District troughs have been eroded along the lines of pre-existing river valleys, which in many cases followed geological faults and fracture zones. Therefore the ice was channelled by the pre-formed topography, and through a combination of plucking and abrasion the river valleys were transformed over successive glacial phases into the troughs we see today. Trough formation would have occurred at times of both valley glaciation and ice-sheet glaciation.

A further influence on trough development is the process of **pressure release**. During the withdrawal of glaciers from valleys, the rocks expand

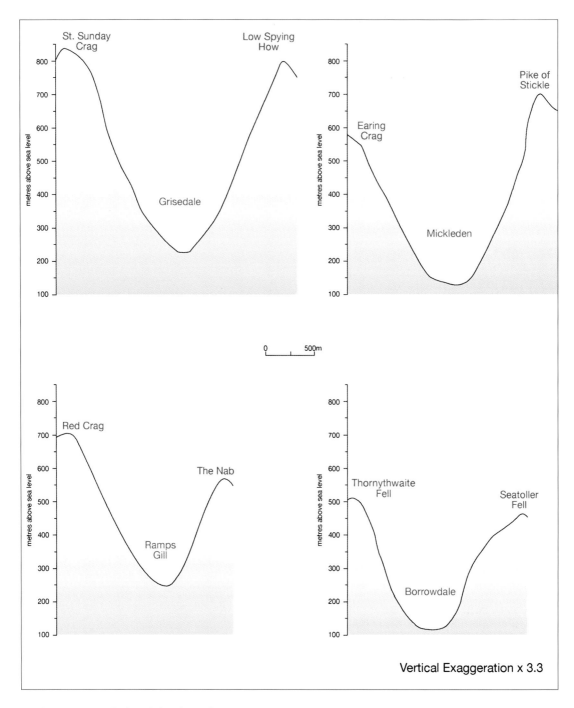

4.6 Cross-sections of selected glacial troughs.

as the pressure exerted by the ice is removed. This leads to the development of rock fractures that trend parallel to the ground surface and creates a body of weakened rock that facilitates erosion in the next glacial phase. On steep valley sides pressure release can result in slope failures (see Chapter 6); these provide vast quantities of rock debris for entrainment and transport by future glaciers.

Glacial troughs often exhibit areas of localised **overdeepening**. These are zones where the floor of the trough has been eroded more deeply into the rock than in adjacent areas. They can be accounted for by geological factors and/or changes in the thickness or velocity of the ice. All Lake District troughs have these basins. The larger/deeper basins are occupied by lakes or tarns, some of the smaller/shallower ones have been infilled with mineral sediment or peat and may be difficult to recognise, although their flat or slightly raised surfaces and susceptibility to flooding after heavy rain give them away.

Major lakes now occupy the most impressive of the overdeepenings. Wast Water, a single basin, is 76 m deep and extends 15 m below present sea level (4.7). Windermere is divided into two basins (north and south)

4.7 Wast Water exists because the valley has undergone serious overdeepening.

separated by Belle Isle and the neighbouring shallows. These basins exceed 100 m in depth and, again, are excavated to below sea level. In contrast, Little Langdale Tarn and Watendlath Tarn occupy much smaller and shallower areas of overdeepening.

By taking lake depth and height of flanking mountains it is possible to estimate the maximum amount of glacial erosion that has occurred. For several troughs this is of the order of 600–700 m but the true figure is likely to be somewhat less because it includes an unknown amount of erosion accomplished by the pre-glacial river. Nevertheless, given that rates of valley erosion by glaciers are of the order of 1 m per 1000 years, there has certainly been sufficient time for Quaternary glaciers to carve out the Lake District valleys. Even if we say that glaciers eroded only one half of the 600–700 m rock thickness, it is still a substantial amount of erosion.

There are several other features associated with glacial troughs that are best considered under this heading rather than being treated separately. One such landscape element is the **truncated spur**. Prior to glaciation, the valleys are likely to have had sinuous courses due to variations in rock character and the nature of water flow. During glacial episodes valley-side spurs were gradually planed back by glacial erosion to give steep buttresses, which now project boldly from valley sides, and straighter valleys. The truncated spurs on the south side of Blencathra are probably the best known in Lakeland, but many other examples can be seen on the sides of most troughs. 4.8 shows three such spurs in Deepdale.

Where a glacial trough was excavated to a depth that is greater than that of a tributary trough, the floor of the latter became perched at a higher level and is known as a **hanging valley**. The length of time the valleys were occupied by glaciers, the erosive power of the ice, and local geological factors may account for some of these hanging relationships. However, other hanging valleys may have developed as the drainage system evolved prior to glaciation. If that is so then glacial erosion has maintained the relationship between valleys.

In several cases the height difference between the main trough and its hanging tributary is considerable and the stream issuing from the latter forms a spectacular waterfall or series of cascades. The Lake District is well endowed with hanging valleys, and many of the large waterfalls and cascades are indicative of their presence. Several such valleys are to be found in Borrowdale (4.9): the valleys of Styhead Gill (Taylorgill Force), Hause Gill, Comb Gill, and Watendlath Beck (Lodore Falls) all hang above the main valley. Mosedale (Ritson's Force) hangs with respect to Wasdale, Little Langdale (Colwith Force) with respect to Great Langdale, upper Easedale (Sourmilk Gill) with respect to Far Easedale, Grisedale with respect to Patterdale, Fordingdale (Measand Force) with respect to Mardale. These are just a few of the many examples.

Obstructions to the efficient flow of valley glaciers can occur due to the vagaries of terrain, geology and nearby ice masses, and when this happens an advancing glacier will thicken and may rise higher than an existing low point on its confining ridges. This thickening can occur at the head of the valley as well as some distance from the head, and if the upper layers of ice begin to flow across the low point into the adjacent valley the glacier is said to have breached its watershed or drainage divide. The area of breaching is called a **spillway** or **diffluent col** and the process is known as **glacial diffluence**. Some glacier ice from Great Langdale flowed into Little Langdale via the Blea Tarn col (4.10) and some from Grasmere went across Red Bank into Great Langdale. Part of the Patterdale glacier crossed Boredale Hause, and some Borrowdale ice found an escape route

4.8 A trio of truncated spurs in Deepdale. From left to right, Greenhow End, Hutaple Crag and Black Buttress.

4.9 Taylorgill Force (centre) marks the place where the hanging valley of Styhead Gill meets upper Borrowdale.

4.10 The lowest point on the skyline ridge is the Blea Tarn col. The Great Langdale glacier breached its watershed here and ice flowed into Little Langdale. As a consequence the col was eroded and lowered somewhat.

over Puddingstone Bank above Rosthwaite to the Watendlath valley. These are examples of breaching along valley sides. Some of the ice that accumulated on the Borrowdale side of Honister Pass went west to Buttermere, ice in the Thirlmere trough passed over Dunmail Raise to Grasmere, and Patterdale ice breached Kirkstone Pass; all are examples of valley head breaching. These patterns of glacier movement are known because indicators of ice-flow direction such as **roches moutonnées** and **erratics** provide the evidence. One result of glacial diffluence was to erode and thereby lower the cols but by how much any one col was lowered is difficult to determine.

Cirques

Cirques are armchair-shaped, mountainside hollows that have been excavated by glacier ice. They possess steep headwalls and sidewalls, usually with cliffs, and more gently sloping floors, that may contain small lakes or peat bogs. When seen from above, a cirque headwall is arcuate and is continued by the sidewalls, resulting in a roughly semi-circular plan form. In Scotland, cirques are known as **corries**, in Wales as **cwms,** and in the Lake District as **coves** and **comb(e)s**, as in Nethermost Cove and Burtness Comb, although some have no official name and are called with respect to a local feature – for example, Blea Water Cove on High Street and Hause Moss Cove on Fairfield.

Many cirques are perched high on the sides of mountains (4.11a) and their streams form impressive waterfalls and cascades as they flow over the lip and descend to the valley floor below; in this respect these cirques are similar to hanging valleys. Other cirques occur at the head of glacial troughs (4.11b) and may not have such a pronounced lip and associated plunging stream.

It is usually assumed that cirques develop from pre-existing mountainside hollows, created perhaps by stream erosion or landsliding. These hollows provide some degree of shelter for the accumulation of snow and ice in cold episodes; as a result small glaciers develop there. The glaciers gradually enlarge the hollows by both plucking and abrasion; enlargement is also aided by freeze-thaw weathering of bedrock around the margins of the glacier. Over successive glacial phases cirques grow in size. As they grow they can trap and hold more snow, which results in larger glaciers that are likely to accomplish more erosion.

At times of extensive glaciation, cirque glaciers may flow beyond the cirque lip and join with other ice masses to form a valley glacier. At other

4.11 a, The cirques of Ruthwaite Cove (left) and Nethermost Cove (right) are perched high above Grisedale; b, Rydale Head, a cirque at the head of a glacial trough.

times cirque glaciers may be augmented by ice spilling over the headwall from a high plateau source. So the enlargement of cirques occurs during all stages of glaciation – from when glaciers are small and restricted to the cirques to when glaciers fill and expand beyond the confines of the cirques. As with glacial troughs, the Lake District cirques have developed over successive glacial phases.

Cirques differ enormously in size, ranging from hillside niches that may be only 50 m in length and width to features whose dimensions exceed 1 km. In terms of morphology, cirques can be of classical form, as described above, or more open, less-enclosed features in which headwalls and sidewalls are not very well developed. In addition, the floor of a cirque can dip inwards or outwards. These differences are due to geological factors, the amount of time over which glaciers have occupied the cirques, and the ability of the ice to erode and transform the initial hollow into a typical cirque.

Some mountains possess a single cirque while others may have several that have been deeply excavated and have reduced the mountains to steep-sided peaks or indented plateaux with summits now linked by narrow ridges. In some areas small cirques occur within larger cirques and result from periods when climatic conditions permitted only very small glaciers to develop in the most sheltered of sites in the existing cirques. Over time minor cirques have been excavated into parts of major cirques.

Climate also controls the directions that cirques face. In the mid-latitudes of the northern hemisphere most cirques face between north and east. This is for two reasons. First, these aspects receive less solar radiation and therefore provide snow and ice with greater protection from melting and, second, for many mountains these directions are on their leeward sides and they receive more snow as a result of it being blown from the windward sides by strong winds.

The cirques of the Lake District have been counted and categorised by Dr Ian Evans. He identified 158, although 35 of these were thought to be of doubtful status and origin. The majority (125) of the cirques are on Borrowdale rocks, 28 are on Skiddaw rocks and 5 are on the Ennerdale Granite. Cirques only occur on fells with a summit height in excess of 450 m, and directions between north and east have been most favoured for their development. The average dimensions are: width 680 m, length 620 m, and depth 270 m. Some mountains have a single cirque (e.g. Lonscale Fell has Lonscale Cove), others have several (e.g. Pillar has five, Scafell has four); some cirques contain tarns (e.g. Blea Water Cove) others contain peat bogs (e.g. Gavel Moss Cove on St. Sunday Crag). Small cirques occur in several of the larger cirques (e.g. White Cove in Burtness Comb, and Chapel Crags Cove in Bleaberry Tarn Comb). Burtness Comb, Bleaberry Tarn Comb and Ling Comb hang above Buttermere, as does Gillercomb above Seathwaite in Borrowdale, other cirques occupy trough heads (e.g. the back-to-back cirques of Threshthwaite Cove in the Pasture Beck valley and Stony Cove at the head of the Trout Beck valley). The morphological contrasts displayed by Lake District cirques reflect the initial differences in the form of the original mountainside hollows, the local geology and the work of the glaciers. Thus, the cirques display great variation in size, shape and setting (4.11).

Major features associated with cirques are **tarns** and **arêtes**. **Tarns** occupy areas of localised overdeepening on cirque floors and will be treated in more detail in Chapter 7. **Arêtes** are narrow and precipitous rock ridges created by glacial erosion. Where an arête projects above the ice surface during a glacial interval, freeze-thaw weathering will also play a part in its formation by shattering and sharpening the crest. Arêtes can develop from the ridges that separate side-by-side cirques and from the headwalls of back-to-back cirques. Striding Edge, Swirral Edge and Sharp Edge are excellent examples of the former (4.12). Headwall arêtes are less common; Mickledore may be the best that Lakeland can offer. A few more episodes of intensive cirque glaciation are required to reduce the width of several ridges such as Prison Band on Swirl How, Long Stile on

High Street, Fairfield and Red Pike (Wasdale), and provide some more exciting arêtes.

To get a flavour of Lake District cirques, take the path from Buttermere to Bleaberry Tarn. As you approach the tarn, the meaning of

4.12 Striding Edge – the finest sidewall arête in Lakeland separates Red Tarn Cove (left) from Nethermost Cove (right).

LAKE DISTRICT MOUNTAIN LANDFORMS

a hanging cirque will become apparent, although it was probably so from the village. Continue up from the tarn to Red Pike, and then follow the ridge along to High Stile and High Crag. The ridge route provides you with a bird's eye view of the major and minor cirques that bite deeply into this mountain wall. Another fine cirque-spotting route is from Patterdale or Glenridding to Red Tarn beneath Helvellyn. Standing by the tarn, you are in one of the finest Lake District cirques. The summit of Helvellyn is at the top of the headwall; the arêtes of Striding Edge and Swirral Edge form the sidewalls. The walk south from Helvellyn, along the eastern edge of Nethermost Pike, High Crag and Dollywaggon Pike to Grisedale Tarn gives another dramatic aerial perspective of several hanging cirques.

Ice-Scoured Terrain

This term does not refer to a specific landform; rather it applies to an area of the landscape made up of an assemblage of features that give rise to a very distinctive topography. Ice-scoured terrain is composed of numerous rock knolls, **roches moutonnées**, and small hollows and overdeepened basins. The amount of erosion has not necessarily been great but the ice has accentuated the irregularities in the bedrock, and the height difference between knolls and depressions is usually a few tens of metres. Hollows and basins occupy areas where the rock joint density is high or where the rock is less resistant to erosion; knolls form where the rock has proved to be of greater resistance to erosion. David Linton referred to the ice-scoured areas of northwest Scotland as **knock and lochan** terrain.

The Lake District also has extensive areas of such topography. One tract is that from Coniston Water by Windermere to the Kendal area and is on rocks of the Windermere Supergroup. Zones of scouring on the Borrowdale Volcanic Group include the Dunnerdale fells above Ulpha, the Yewdale fells above Coniston, and the summits of Loughrigg Fell, Haystacks, Grange Fell, Rosthwaite Fell and Seathwaite Fell, to name just a few (4.13). Another area, underlain by the Ennerdale Granite, is alongside the road to Wasdale Head around its junction with the Greendale turning. In Eskdale, Eel Tarn and Stony Tarn and numerous other wet peaty hollows occupy scoured terrain on the local granite. Areal scouring is not as common on rocks of the Skiddaw Group because they tend to be of a more homogeneous nature, but evidence for slight scouring is present on the summits of Barf, Rannerdale Knotts and Causey Pike.

Ice-scoured terrain is usually very rough and intricate, and if lacking in paths can be awkward to traverse. The name Knott or Knotts, meaning

4.13 Ice-scoured terrain is evident in this view of Rosthwaite Fell from the summit of High Raise.

a craggy, compact hill, has been used for some of these areas, and their diversity and complexity were recognised by Wainwright.

He said, about the summit of Haystacks – '...the combination of features, of tarn and tor, of cliff and cove, the labyrinth of corners and recesses, the maze of old sheepwalks and paths, form a design, or lack of design, of singular appeal and absorbing interest.' (A. Wainwright 1966, *The Western Fells*).

About Great Crag, between Watendlath and Stonethwaite, he wrote – '...an indefinite and complex mass of rough undulating ground, a place of craggy and wooded slopes, of heathery tors and mossy swamps and shy little tarns – a beautiful labyrinth, a joy to the explorer but the despair of the map-maker.' (A. Wainwright 1958, *The Central Fells*).

Roches Moutonnées

Roches moutonnées are very common landforms in the Lake District. They can be found on the floors and flanks of glaciated valleys and cirques, and are a major component of terrain that was subjected to areal scouring. They are defined as bedrock knolls or hills with an asymmetric profile. Such a profile results from glacial **abrasion** on the side that faces the direction from which the ice came (i.e. the up-ice side), and glacial **plucking** on the side facing the direction the ice was going (i.e. the down-ice side). The result is a knoll or hill with a smooth, rounded and gently inclined up-ice face and a steep, craggy down-ice face (4.14). These features can range from a few metres in length and height to tens or hundreds of metres, and they frequently occur in groups. The majority of Lake District examples are up to several tens of metres in length and height.

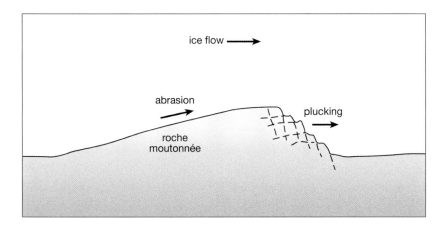

4.14 Sketch showing the morphology of a roche moutonnée and the areas of abrasion and plucking.

The general consensus regarding the formation of roches moutonnées is that they result from differences in pressure between the up-ice and down-ice sides of a pre-existing bedrock knoll. Higher than average pressures occur on the up-ice face of a knoll as a glacier flows across it, and this favours abrasion. As the glacier passes over the top of the knoll, pressures fall to below average, and a cavity opens as the ice separates from the rock. Within the cavity, rock fracturing is encouraged by the presence and pressure of meltwater and because of freezing and thawing. Once blocks have been loosened they can be carried away (plucking) by the adjacent ice.

Roches moutonnées are very common in areas underlain by Borrowdale and Windermere rocks, but are not as prevalent on Skiddaw rocks. Excellent examples occur in Grasmere village – one is at the entrance to the car park beside the village hall; Rothay Park in Ambleside has some, Borrowdale has a lot. Many of those that occur on valley floors are surrounded and partly covered by trees, but there is no doubting their origin (4.15a). Where trees are absent, as on many high level areas of scoured terrain, roche moutonnée morphology is unmistakeable (4.15b). One clue to their presence in the landscape is the name How or Howe,

4.15 a, A tree-covered roche moutonnée by the roadside in Borrowdale. Ice flow was from left to right; b, A roche moutonnée in an area of ice-scoured terrain; Little Round How above Warnscale Bottom. Ice flow was from right to left.

meaning a hill or mound, usually of modest size. Not all How(e)s are roches moutonnées, but many are – such as The How at Rosthwaite, and Great Round How and Little Round How above Warnscale Bottom.

As to the French name – wavy wigs were fashionable in the eighteenth century and were known as *moutonnées* because mutton fat was used to keep them in shape. The name was adopted for knolls and hills that had a likeness to the wigs – hence, roches (rock) moutonnées.

Meltwater Channels

Whether glaciers are waxing or waning, **meltwater** will be present in various quantities and in various places. Some water will flow alongside the margins of the ice and some will flow beneath the ice. Other water will flow on or within the ice. These pathways of water movement are usually interconnected such that water flowing adjacent to the ice margin may suddenly find itself diverted to inside or below the glacier because a crevasse or cavity has opened up. Once within the glacier, the water may find its way to the base of the ice where it becomes part of the subglacial meltwater. Water on the ice surface may be routed to the glacier edge to join with the marginal flow. Eventually meltwater will reach the leading edge of the ice and from there it flows away. As glaciers and ice-sheets enlarge and then ultimately waste away, the routes taken by meltwater will change accordingly.

In all these positions the water will carry sediment and may excavate a channel for itself. As glaciers melt, channels carved into the ice surface gradually vanish but channels that were eroded alongside, beneath and in front of glaciers are usually preserved because they are in bedrock or thick sediment. These channels are very distinctive landforms and are named from their former location in relation to the ice. So we recognise **ice-marginal channels** (alongside the ice), **subglacial channels** (beneath the ice) and **proglacial channels** (in front of the ice), but which is which can sometimes be difficult to establish because similarities can exist between channels formed in different positions. Meltwater channels are identified from their profile characteristics, from their position in the landscape, from their large depth and width in relation to their present-day stream, or because they no longer contain flowing water and are dry channels.

The morphology of **ice-marginal channels** can be rather varied. They can start and stop abruptly. A bowl-shaped niche on a hillside may mark the beginning of such a channel and is usually taken to indicate the point where water cascaded from a glacier surface and impact erosion occurred. Leading from the niche a straight or sinuous channel may cut across the hillside for some distance before turning sharply downslope at a right angle and disappearing. This point is taken to mark where the water entered the ice via a crevasse or cavity, or went back onto the ice surface. If the water went below the ice, rather than into or onto it, the marginal channel may be continued by a **subglacial channel** or **chute**.

Some ice-marginal channels are actually only 'half channels', that is to say they look like a bench or step extending across a hillside. In these cases the outer wall of the 'channel' was the glacier itself, which has long since gone. Where the position of the glacier margin fluctuated over time, a flight of closely spaced, sub-parallel marginal channels may have been created and now give the hillside a stepped or corrugated appearance.

In contrast to ice-marginal meltwater, which is gravity-driven flow, subglacial meltwater may be under great pressure (hydrostatic pressure), which can cause it to flow uphill. Where this has happened, the long profile of the resulting channel is characteristically undulating and is known as an up-and-down profile. Such channel profiles are indicative of erosion by pressurised subglacial meltwater and are a key factor in the recognition of their subglacial origin.

Some subglacial channels may have continued to carry water after the ice retreated. In doing so they became **proglacial channels** and then the channels for the post-glacial rivers. The gorge sections that characterise several rivers may owe their origin to vigorous erosion by enormous quantities of subglacial meltwater heavily charged with sediment, but it is impossible to know how much of this erosion was subglacial, how much was proglacial and how much has been due to post-glacial river activity. River gorges range in scale from that at Wallabarrow in Dunnerdale (about 1 km long, 250 m wide and 150 m deep) to that at Stockley Bridge above Seathwaite in Borrowdale (about 50 m long, 6 m wide and 10 m deep).

Meltwater channels have been recorded in several parts of the Lake District; in other parts they are seemingly absent, but this may be because they haven't yet been recognised in those areas. Splendid examples occur on the fells south of Ennerdale Bridge, including the very impressive Nannycatch Gorge. The western end of Muncaster Fell has channels cut across it and, to the south, the lower slopes of Corney Fell, between 70–150 m, are notched by many channels. A series of channels is present on Aughertree Fell, on the northern margin of the National Park (4.16a). This set is particularly accessible because the minor road from Uldale to Caldbeck passes within a few hundreds of metres and there is convenient roadside parking. Other channels occupy the area southeast of Little Mell Fell, between Watermillock church and Bennethead. A further collection of channels can be found crossing the top and northern slopes of Threlkeld Knotts, below the steep north-west slopes of Clough Head. It is possible to pick these channels out by the contour crenellations on the 1:25,000 scale OS map. One channel

4.16 a, A large meltwater channel cuts across part of Aughertree Fell; b, This small meltwater channel on Threlkeld Knotts is crossed by the Old Coach Road (middle left).

(4.16b) is crossed by the Old Coach Road from St. John's in the Vale to Matterdale.

You may have noticed that I haven't said which types of meltwater channel occur at these places – that's for you to work out!

Striations and Friction Cracks

Glacial erosion creates an assortment of superficial markings on rock surfaces. Of these markings, probably the most common are **striations** and **friction cracks**. Although of widespread occurrence, they may be absent from some rock surfaces either because they never formed there or because subsequent weathering and erosion have removed them. The up-ice, abraded, faces of roches moutonnées are appropriate places to search for these features.

Striations are scratch marks that form when particles embedded in the base of a glacier are dragged across rock surfaces, or when particles in the ice come into direct contact and move relative to one another. They are therefore a result of **abrasion**. Although striations are usually very shallow features (a few millimetres at most) they can be several metres in length.

On bedrock surfaces, striations usually have a common orientation and are taken to indicate a single episode of ice flow (4.17a). Two or more sets of striations may sometimes be found on the same surface and these are generally regarded as representing separate ice flow episodes or a change in the pattern of ice movement. Careful examination of the striations and their cross-cutting relationships may enable determination of the earlier/later set. One implication of cross-cutting striations is that abrasion by the later ice flow event was not sufficient to destroy the striations created by the earlier event. Cross-cutting striations are fairly common on rock fragments contained in glacial deposits (4.17b); when these particles were carried along in the ice they underwent rotation and came into contact with many other fragments. Trackside exposures in glacial sediments will usually reveal striated stones.

The orientation of striations on bedrock surfaces does not tell in which direction the ice was moving. Striations oriented east-west may have been created by ice moving from the east or from the west. Other evidence is required in order to establish the direction of ice flow.

The term **friction cracks** covers a range of features created by small-scale fracturing and plucking of bedrock surfaces. They form because large fragments of rock, carried in the ice, exert an impact pressure on coming

4.17 a, Striations and friction cracks on bedrock. b, Cross-cutting striations on a piece of Skiddaw Group rock taken from a moraine. In both photographs the scale bar divisions are 5 cm. c, Arcuate scars on a slab of Borrowdale Volcanic Group rock. The lens cap diameter is 7 cm.

into direct contact with bedrock. The fractures form as a series of small arcuate scars or grooves (4.17c) and are created when small chips of rock are removed from the surface. Friction cracks are often found along with striations on the same rock surface (4.17a). Friction cracks differ from striations in that contact between the rock fragment in the ice and the bedrock surface is not continuous. Rather, cracks result from intermittent rock-on-rock contact.

Glacial deposition

The material eroded by glaciers is carried away from its place of origin as the ice flows across the landsurface. A glacier transports eroded materials at its base (known as **subglacial transport**), within the ice (**englacial transport**), and on its surface (**supraglacial transport**). As glaciers move, these materials do not always remain in the same position. Supraglacial debris may fall or be washed into crevasses; it then becomes part of the englacial or subglacial material. In some glaciers, compressive forces can cause ice and debris to be thrust forwards and upwards towards the surface so that englacial and subglacial materials move into the supraglacial zone (4.18). Just to confuse things a little, some supraglacial debris may not have been eroded by ice at all – rather, it could have fallen onto the glacier surface from valley side crags above the ice – and can become part of the englacial and subglacial debris as described above. Furthermore, as glaciers undergo melting the supraglacial debris is supplemented by debris that has melted out from the englacial zone (4.19).

Ultimately, all these materials are deposited. Glacial deposition occurs as the ice is moving, when it becomes stationary, and during its decay. Some debris is deposited directly by the ice and is generally known as

4.18 Long-section sketch of a glacier showing different types of debris (supraglacial, englacial and subglacial) and their transport paths.

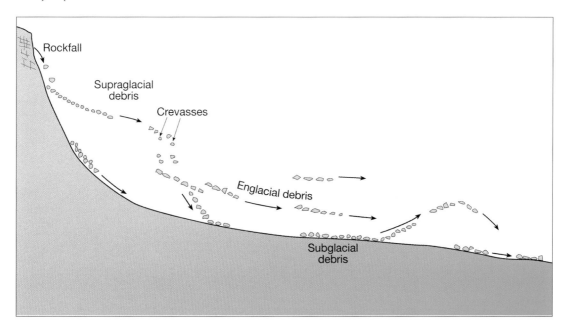

glacial till; other debris is carried, sorted and deposited by meltwater, in which case it is called **glacifluvial sediment**. Many of the glacial and glacifluvial deposits have a distinct morphology that enables them to be categorised according to how they were deposited and where in relation to the glacier they were deposited. So, we recognise landforms created by **subglacial deposition** (beneath the ice), **supraglacial** and **englacial deposition** (from on or within the ice), **ice-marginal deposition** (alongside the ice), and **proglacial deposition** (in front of the ice). Some of these terms were used previously in relation to meltwater channels.

As was mentioned earlier in this chapter, the deposits of three episodes of glaciation are known to exist in the Lake District. However, the earliest deposits are deeply buried below the surface, so the depositional landforms that we see were created during one or other of the last two glacial episodes. These occurred between 25,000 and 15,000 years ago when a large ice-sheet developed over most of Scotland, Wales and northern England (the Late Devensian Glaciation), and between 13,000 and 11,500 years ago when British glaciers were of restricted extent and, in the Lake District, occupied the cirques, valley heads and some high plateau areas (the Loch Lomond Glaciation).

Because the areas covered by glaciers in the Loch Lomond episode are fairly well known, we are able to say which of the landforms of glacial deposition were created at that time and which relate to the more extensive Late Devensian Glaciation.

4.19 The terminal zone of this glacier in the Swiss Alps is covered with debris derived from supraglacial sources and englacial meltout.

Landforms of glacial deposition

Drumlins

The word **drumlin** comes from *druim* – a Gaelic (Irish) word for a rounded hill. More specifically, a drumlin is a smooth, oval or elliptical hill between about 5 and 50 m in height and from 10 to 3000 m in length. In plan view they resemble the bowl of an upturned dessert spoon or an egg turned on its side and half-buried. One end of a drumlin is usually blunt and steep; the other end normally tapers and is less steep. These are known respectively as the stoss slope and the lee slope.

Drumlins typically occur in great swarms known as **drumlin fields,** which may contain tens, hundreds or thousands of individuals. Such concentrations, along with their morphology when seen in plan view, have given rise to the term **basket of eggs topography.** However, whereas eggs in a basket may be arranged so as to point in different directions, drumlins in a drumlin field tend to be aligned in the same direction. This alignment is parallel to the direction in which the ice was moving – the stoss slope faces in the up-ice direction and the lee slope faces in the down-ice direction – therefore drumlins are very useful indicators of the routes taken by long-vanished glaciers and ice-sheets. Because of their shape and alignment, drumlins are regarded as a type of **streamlined landform.**

Although the origin of drumlins has been the focus of much research, it may be wrong to think of them in terms of a single universal mechanism. Many theories have been proposed to account for their formation but there is little consensus among geomorphologists. The concept of **equifinality** that we met with in Chapter 1 may be appropriate with respect to drumlins.

However, we do know that drumlins form beneath glaciers and ice-sheets and are therefore of subglacial origin, but they do not form everywhere in the subglacial zone. We also know, from many road cuttings and quarries in drumlins, that they can be composed of different materials. Some are made up entirely of glacial till, some are predominantly of water-sorted sands and gravels, some have layers of both till and sands and gravels, and others have a core of bedrock that is covered with one or both of the aforementioned materials. It is no wonder that many hypotheses have been advanced to explain them!

The plethora of ideas can be grouped into those that consider drumlins to result from erosion of ice and sediment, and those that consider them to result from sediment deposition. It is probably true to say that the erosional theories have less support among geomorphologists than the depositional theories. If it had been the other way around then I would have placed this section under the heading **Landforms of Glacial Erosion**, earlier in the chapter.

Drumlin formation by erosion could take one of two forms. First, the ice or subglacial meltwater may erode depressions in a pre-existing layer of thick sediment and so create a series of hillocks that are then shaped by ice movement. Second, it is known that large lakes exist in places beneath glaciers and ice-sheets, and it has been proposed that in past glacial episodes **outburst floods** from similar subglacial lakes may have scoured the base of the ice and created large cavities that were later infilled with glacial till or water-sorted sediments. This latter idea is known as the **megaflood hypothesis** and stems from investigations undertaken in Canada.

The most plausible explanation associating drumlins with sediment deposition concerns a process known as **subglacial deformation**. This involves ice moving over a sediment layer that, in some parts, readily deforms due to the pressure exerted by the ice. The deformable sediment is said to undergo moulding around obstacles such as bedrock knolls, concentrations of boulders, and masses of stiffer sediment that do not deform. In this way hillocks of sediment develop beneath the ice and are shaped in the direction of ice flow. Many geomorphologists now favour this mechanism but there are some who still do not. No doubt the debate will continue.

Drumlins are not very well represented in the Lake District and where present they are in rather small groups. Nevertheless, examples occur in the vicinity of Ings, between Staveley and Windermere, and these are well seen from the summit of Reston Scar (4.20); in the valley of Esthwaite Water and Cunsey Beck, where some form shoreline promontories known as 'Ees'; between Grizedale and Satterthwaite in Grizedale Forest; and Keswick is built on and around drumlins, with the clearest one being occupied by Crow Park, opposite the town's theatre. In each of these cases an examination of the contours on the relevant 1:25,000 scale OS map will reveal the shape and extent of the drumlins.

If you want to see more extensive drumlin fields with large individuals then you will have to go outside of the National Park to one or more of the following areas – between Lancaster and Kendal, to the north of Penrith, to the Eden valley north from Kirkby Stephen, to the Solway plain around Wigton, or to the area between Ulverston and Barrow-in-Furness – all have drumlins in abundance. Again, the contour patterns

4.20 Extending across the centre of the photograph is one of the drumlins at Ings. Other drumlins occur to the right of the white farmhouse in the background. The viewpoint is Reston Scar.

on the OS maps are a clue to their locations. All of these places, and those mentioned above that are within the Lake District, were last covered by glacier ice during the Late Devensian Glaciation and it was during that episode that the drumlins were formed.

Why is the Lake District deficient in drumlins relative to the areas surrounding it? There are several possible reasons, but obviously subglacial conditions beneath Lake District glaciers were simply not conducive to drumlin development. This may have been because the subglacial sediment was not deformable, or because subglacial lakes and megafloods did not occur, or that the glaciers were constricted in their movement and were not moving fast enough. Drumlin fields have often been associated with high rates of ice flow and this is likely to have been the case in the lowland areas adjacent to the Lake District mountains.

Moraines

Moraines are ridges and mounds of glacial debris, and are probably the most abundant type of landform resulting from glacial deposition in the Lake District. They are present in most of the valleys and cirques and can be of different types, sizes and extents along the length of a valley. Some moraines are regarded as ice-marginal landforms and are very useful in that they enable the changing configurations and positions of glaciers to be determined during deglaciation. Other moraines derive from debris carried on and in the ice and result from supraglacial and englacial deposition.

There are different ways in which moraines can be classified. One commonly used system is based on the processes that caused debris to accumulate; this is frequently applied to moraines that are forming on and around glaciers today and where the processes can be seen to be oper-ating or their rates can be measured. Accordingly, **thrust moraines, push moraines, dump moraines** and **ablation moraines** are recognised. In areas where glaciers no longer exist, the terminology is usually related to the position of moraines in the landscape and their location in relation to the former glaciers. So, we refer to **terminal (end) moraines, recessional moraines, lateral moraines** and **medial moraines**. Another way in which moraines are categorised is by reference to their morphology; terms such as **hummocky moraines, arcuate moraines** and **saw-tooth moraines** are in common usage.

In spite of having different criteria with which to classify moraines, not all moraines fit neatly into one or other of these categories. Some moraines may result from more than one formative process and there-fore they are composite features. Evidence for the processes that created moraines is often to be found in the characteristics of the debris itself, but in the Lake District most moraines are covered by vegetation and there are very few exposures that allow us to 'see inside'. For this reason, Lake District moraines are best referred to by their location in relation to the former glaciers and/or their morphology.

Moraines that occupy the cirques and upper reaches of Lake District valleys are generally ascribed to the Loch Lomond Glaciation. Elsewhere in the valleys, moraines are regarded as having formed as the ice of the Late Devensian Glaciation wasted away. However, very few moraines have been dated.

When using morphology to categorise Lake District moraines it must be remembered that in some cases 11,500 years have passed since the

4.21 a, This is one of three moraine ridges (one terminal and two recessional) that cross the valley floor at Rosthwaite in Borrowdale. In this case the steeper and concave face results from erosion by the River Derwent. Ice flow was from left to right; b, The last glacier to occupy the Bowscale Tarn cirque built up the large terminal moraine ridge on the right of the tarn; c. Lateral moraine ridges at the foot of Stake Pass in Langstrath; d, Hummocky moraine at the head of Mickleden.

moraines were created, in other cases about 15,000 years have elapsed, and substantial changes to moraine morphology and size are likely to have occurred. Rivers and streams have undoubtedly eroded parts of many moraines.

Four types of moraine are commonly encountered in the Lake District.

Terminal or End moraines form around the maximum downvalley extent (snout) of a glacier and usually have an arcuate plan form with the concave side facing up-ice. Some terminal moraines are broadly arcuate; others form a much tighter arc. The nature of the concavity can be taken as indicating the plan form morphology of the glacier snout. Thrusting, pushing, or dumping of debris, or some combination of these processes can create a terminal moraine at the limit of a cirque or valley glacier. Where the ice margin was stationary for a considerable time, or if the glacier was carrying a considerable debris load, a large terminal moraine may have formed. The withdrawal of a glacier from a terminal moraine may be followed by stillstands of the ice front or by readvances. Moraines created at these times are known as **recessional moraines** and are subjected to the same set of processes as was the terminal moraine.

Excellent examples of a terminal moraine and two recessional moraine ridges can be seen at Rosthwaite in Borrowdale (4.21a). The vicarage and campsite are situated among the ridges and several footpaths cross them. The River Derwent has cut into the moraines at several places opposite Longthwaite (Borrowdale Youth Hostel). Another terminal moraine occurs a short distance up-valley at Thorneythwaite. The farm sits on top of the moraine, and the footpath from Strands Bridge to Seathwaite crosses part of the moraine that is still strewn with large boulders. The Rosthwaite moraines mark the limit of the glacier from the Stonethwaite valley (a combination of ice from Langstrath and Greenup); the Thorneythwaite moraine was formed at the snout of the Seathwaite glacier. Several cirques also have well-developed terminal moraines. Two of the largest are at Bowscale Tarn (4.21b) and Wolf Crags. The Old Coach Road from St. John's in the Vale to Matterdale runs along the crest of the latter moraine (known as Barbary Rigg). Other clear examples are at Red Tarn (Helvellyn), Blea Water and Bleaberry Tarn. The absence of terminal moraines from some Lake District cirques and valleys may be because conditions did not permit their development or because erosion has reduced them to mere fragments of their former selves, making them difficult to recognise.

As with terminal moraines, lateral moraines also develop in ice-marginal positions. They occupy the areas alongside cirque and valley glaciers and may connect to a terminal moraine. Laterals form mainly due to the dumping of glacial debris – the debris falls, slides or flows from the surface of the ice. Some debris in laterals can accumulate by rockfall from crags on valley sides above the glacier. Where this happens, the moraine is composed of materials from different sources. Although lateral moraines can form on both sides of a glacier, a marked difference in their relative sizes may be evident. If one side of the valley has a greater extent of crags, rockfall debris may have made a major contribution to lateral moraine development on that side.

Glaciers become thinner and narrower as they melt. A new set of lateral moraines may then develop – recessional laterals. These moraine ridges are protected to some extent from the accumulation of rockfall debris by the laterals higher on the valley side. In some situations lateral moraines may not be present because powerful ice-marginal meltwater flows may have removed the debris almost as quickly as it accumulated.

Many of the lateral moraines in the Lake District are rather subdued features but 'getting your eye in' with some clear examples should enable you to recognise some less prominent ones later. Good places to see well developed laterals are on the east-facing hillside above Hayeswater Gill, south of Hayeswater, on the south-facing slopes of Mickleden, on the north-facing hillside just below the summit of Honister Pass on the Borrowdale side, at the foot of Stake Pass in Langstrath (4.21c), and in Nethermost Cove and Ruthwaite Cove above Grisedale.

The term hummocky moraine is used for areas of moraine mounds and depressions that have a seemingly disorganised or chaotic appearance. Hummock development is favoured where a melting glacier is covered by an extensive amount of thick debris. As melting proceeds irregularly the debris cover assumes a hummocky appearance and material slumps or flows from the steep-sided hummocks into the depressions, so causing localised changes to the debris thickness and the surface topography. When the ice eventually disappears the debris is left behind with a hummocky morphology.

Hummocky moraines can be seen in several Lake District cirques and valleys – the upper reaches of Greenup, Grisedale, above Black Sail Youth Hostel at the head of Ennerdale, in both Deepdales, and in Mickleden (4.21d).

Erratics and Perched Boulders

Jonathan Otley was aware that boulders of Lake District rocks occurred far from their place of origin but was unable to explain why this was so. It was realised later that glaciers had picked up these rocks, carried them away from their source, and deposited them in an area of different geology. Such rocks are known as **erratics** (from *errare* (Latin) meaning 'to go astray'). Traditionally, the term has been used for large boulders that occur some distance away from their place of origin, and their transport can only be explained in terms of carriage by ice. Included within most glacial deposits are small rock fragments that are 'foreign' to their place of deposition, and these can also be considered as erratics.

The Swiss geologist Louis Agassiz used the distribution of erratics to demonstrate that Alpine glaciers had previously been much more extensive. A similar argument for rock transport by former glaciers was presented to explain the occurrence of 'foreign' stones in various parts of Great Britain. Not only do erratics inform us that glaciers previously existed, they can also be used to establish the directions and patterns of ice movement. In this context, erratics from the very distinctive Shap Granite in the east of the Lake District (see Chapter 2) have been used to establish the routes taken by ice crossing this part of Cumbria. The granite erratics show that some ice went across the Pennines via Stainmore Pass and some went down the valley of the River Lune and on into the Midlands.

Erratics can also be used within the Lake District to determine the routes taken by glaciers. For example, as ice flowed north from the Thirlmere valley it carried with it pieces of rock from the Armboth Dyke. In the vicinity of High Rigg and Low Rigg, and the outcrops of the Threlkeld Microgranite at the northern end of St. John's in the Vale, the ice flow began to diverge; some ice moved northwest towards the Bassenthwaite valley (Armboth erratics were found on the summit of Latrigg by Clifton Ward in the 1870s), and some went northeast towards and beyond Threlkeld. The Armboth and Threlkeld erratics have been traced to Mungrisdale, and at Linewath, below the east end of Carrock Fell, they can be found within the gravels exposed in an **esker** (see below).

Many of the large boulders that litter the surfaces of some moraines are also erratics, having been transported some distance from their source outcrops. In some cases, boulders on moraines could have fallen from crags. These are not erratics, but it is not always easy to distinguish them from genuine ones. It is possible that some moraine boulders are actually rockfall boulders; if they occur close to the valley side and there are crags and boulders on the hillside above, be suspicious!

Thomas Hay, writing in the 1940s, reported the occurrence of high-level erratics on several Lake District fells. He described a 'train' of in excess of 50 boulders extending across the northeast spur of High Stile from the edge overlooking Burtness Comb to the edge overlooking Bleaberry Tarn Comb. The boulders were of a distinctive volcanic rock derived from an outcrop on the rim of the spur overlooking Burtness Comb. Another erratic train extends south from the top of Deer Bield

4.22 a, This broad erratic train extends away from Deer Bield Crag in Far Easedale; b, Wainwright's perched boulder near Blackbeck Tarn on Haystacks. The survey pole divisions are 20 cm.

Crag in Far Easedale (4.22a). Not all high-level boulders are necessarily erratics. Some could be the result of local frost action (see Chapter 5) and this origin needs to be discounted before you can claim an erratic.

Many of the high-level erratics take the form of **perched boulders** – so called because they sit on flattish rock slabs and rise above their immediate surroundings. There are numerous examples: the eastern flanks of Ullscarf are well endowed, as is the Crinkle Crags ridge. A perched boulder to the south of Blackbeck Tarn, on Haystacks, was illustrated and commented on by Wainwright (although his remarks were not very complimentary – to women). This boulder is of volcanic rock but it is easy to see that it is distinctly different from the volcanic outcrop on which it is perched and it has clearly been transported to its resting place (4.22b).

Eskers

Meltwater flowing in channels beneath, within, and on glaciers may leave behind accumulations of sand and gravel. If these materials are deposited within the ice or on top of the ice they are gradually lowered to the ground surface as the ice melts. The resulting landform is usually a long, winding and undulating ridge that is known as an **esker** (from the Irish word *eiscir* – meaning 'ridge'). They are landforms of **glacifluvial** origin and can range from just a few hundreds of metres to hundreds of kilometres in length; the longest ones may reach heights of 50 m.

Eskers are very rare landforms in the Lake District, but one can be seen in enclosed land in St. John's in the Vale, about 200 m south of Lowthwaite Farm, and is easily identified by the field barn situated on its eastern side facing the road (4.23a). Another is in open land at Linewath (4.23b). There are small quarries in the Linewath esker that show the nature of the sand and gravel of which it is built, and many of the gravel particles are erratics.

It is likely that eskers were previously more widespread but were destroyed as the ice melted. Even though eskers form as a result of meltwater deposition, they are not immune to erosion by meltwater at a later time during deglaciation.

4.23 a, Esker in St. John's in the Vale; b, Esker at Linewath.

Kames

Meltwater flowing on a glacier surface or alongside the ice can deposit sediment that, when the ice melts, takes the form of a flat-topped and steep-sided mound. These landforms are known respectively as **kames** and **kame terraces**. The word **kame** is of Scottish origin (from *cam* or *kaim* – meaning 'steeply-sloping mound') and formerly incorporated those features that we now call **eskers**. Kames and eskers are commonly found in similar settings and are composed of similar materials (sands and gravels), reflecting their glacifluvial origin. Distinguishing between kames and eskers in the field is not always easy because some of their characteristics are similar.

Kames and kame terraces range in size from in excess of a kilometre in length, up to several hundreds of metres in width, and up to several tens of metres in height. However, they tend to be fragmentary or discontinuous features because of dissection by later meltwater flows.

4.24 On the far side of the nearest drystone wall is one of the Naddle valley kame terraces.

Kame and kettle terrain is the term used by geomorphologists for kames that contain hollows (**kettle holes**) that are either filled with water or have a peat-covered floor. The kettle holes formed because blocks of ice that were buried by sand and gravel deposition eventually melted and the overlying sediment subsided and created a hollow.

Kames and kettles have been recorded at several places in the northern part of the Lake District. Examples can be seen between Calfclose Bay and Brockle Beck, on the eastern shore of Derwent Water, in the Naddle valley (4.24), just to the east of the Castlerigg stone circle, and they also occur in association with the esker at Linewath (see above).

Recognising and understanding how eskers and kames developed is not only interesting in itself but can be used to indicate the pathways taken by glacial meltwater flow.

4.25 Sandur in the Seathwaite branch of Borrowdale.

Sandar

Enormous amounts of sand and gravel are carried by meltwater as it flows away from the margins of glaciers and ice-sheets. Much of the material is deposited within a few kilometres of the ice front and is termed **proglacial** sediment. The **braided rivers** that transport and deposit this debris create fairly flat and broad surfaces that can extend across the full width of the valley floor. Such surfaces are known as **sandar** (singular **sandur**, an Icelandic word); an alternative name is **outwash plain**.

In many modern glacial environments sandar often have a pitted appearance. This is because large blocks of ice, broken from the glacier, were buried within the sediment and then they gradually melted. The 'pits' are kettle holes – just like those that can be found on the surfaces of kames.

The flat floors of the main Lake District valleys may be considered as sandar, although they have been greatly modified and converted to valuable agricultural land by the work of generations of farmers (4.25).

Tailpiece

Because the erosional and depositional effects of glaciation are so apparent in the Lake District it has often been thought that the geomorphology of the area can be explained in terms of glaciation alone – or, to put it another way, other landscape processes and resulting landforms are insignificant. While it may be true that the visual impact of glaciation remains clear, in the millennia that have passed since the last glaciers disappeared many other processes have been at work. Some of these processes are still operating, others no longer so, but together they have modified the glacial landforms and left their own signatures in the landscape.

In the chapters that follow, these processes and landforms will be examined and explained. The theme of glaciers and glaciation will be returned to briefly when and where there is an evident glacial legacy.

CHAPTER FIVE

Periglacial processes and landforms

Introduction

I N SPITE OF CONTAINING THE element 'glacial', the term 'periglacial' will not be a familiar one to many people. The term 'tundra' is probably better known and understood, and while it is true that tundra areas are periglacial in character, they do not constitute the only type of periglacial landscape and so the word is not an entirely appropriate alternative.

In 1909 a Polish geologist, Walery von Lozinski, proposed the word 'periglacial' to describe the frost weathering conditions that were responsible for the production of rock rubbles in the Carpathian Mountains of central Europe. The following year he introduced the idea of a periglacial zone, which encompassed the climatic and geomorphic conditions of those areas that had lain adjacent to the great ice-sheets and glaciers, i.e. the areas that had experienced a severely cold climate but had not been directly affected by glacier ice.

However, considerably before Lozinski's time, Victorian geologists in southern England had attributed widespread sheets of 'rubble drift' to a former and significantly colder climate. Clifton Ward described features in the Lake District that had also required cold conditions in which to develop. Therefore Lozinski provided an umbrella term for a wide variety of cold climate non-glacial processes and landforms, and this formalisation, by means of a single expression for a diverse range of features, stimulated much interest, discussion and investigation.

Today, the study of periglacial processes and landforms comprises a distinct subdivision of geomorphology and the definition proposed by Lozinski has been modified. It is now known that periglacial conditions occur in many regions, some of which are far removed from ice-sheets and glaciers. This means, in effect, that although periglacial processes may dominate different landscapes, the climatic conditions in those areas need not be, and usually are not, identical. Periglacial environments range from low altitude Arctic regions with their polar desert climates, to high altitude mountains with their alpine climates, to the interiors of central Asia and northern Canada with their continental climates. There is no such thing as a single periglacial climate – contrasts abound.

Notwithstanding these differences, many geomorphologists regard periglacial areas as those where **permafrost** exists and, as a consequence, intensive **frost action** prevails. But not everyone accepts this definition. Certain areas of the Earth's surface do not have permafrost and yet they experience severe frosts during the winter season; these regions are regarded as periglacial by some other geomorphologists. So, there are marked differences between the definitions that are used and between the characteristics of the so-called periglacial areas. Moreover, in any periglacial area there are likely to be local climatic variations, especially as altitude is gained or lost, and this may be manifest in the vigour of frost activity and permafrost-related processes, and the degree to which associated landforms have developed.

If you are beginning to think that periglacial areas are rather difficult to delimit – you are correct! There is no escaping the fact. The term has been with us for just over 100 years and has provoked much debate, and it is likely to continue doing so for a long time to come.

Periglacial processes

Many of the landshaping processes that operate in periglacial areas are prevalent in other climatic zones as well. For example, fluvial (river) and aeolian (wind) processes are often important in periglacial regions but they also occur in many other parts of the world where temperatures are significantly higher. The processes that differentiate periglacial areas from non-periglacial ones are those related to permafrost and/or those associated with frost action.

Permafrost is usually defined as ground that remains frozen for two or more consecutive years. At present about 25% of the Earth's land surface is underlain by permafrost – particularly the Arctic and sub-Arctic, where it may reach several hundreds of metres in thickness. During Quaternary cold intervals, large swathes of the now-temperate mid-latitudes had permafrost, including the southern parts of Britain that escaped inundation by glaciers. At these times an additional 20–25% of the Earth's surface was periglacial. Therefore, some 45–50% of the land surface either is or has been subjected to periglacial conditions.

If moisture is abundant during the formation of permafrost it can migrate through the rock and soil to produce distinct masses of ice known as **ground ice**. These ice masses create some very prominent landforms that may retain a surface expression long after the permafrost has decayed.

Where permafrost exists at high elevations in temperate and tropical areas, the temperature in the upper part of the frozen ground may rise above 0°C during the day. In high latitude regions the temperature in the upper part of the permafrost only exceeds 0°C during the spring and summer seasons. This diurnal or seasonal melting usually results in a saturated soil known as the **active layer** that may range from a few centimetres to several metres in thickness. Where there is a perceptible gradient there is a tendency for the wet soil to slide or flow downslope (**gelifluction**), either slowly or rapidly, and create some very distinctive features.

Frost action is freezing and thawing of the ground surface. It occurs both in association with permafrost and without it, and so may be an important activity in its own right. The term is a catch-all for several different processes including **frost wedging**, **frost heave** and **frost creep**, and encompasses the development of different types of **soil ice**, such as **needle ice** (5.1) and **ice lenses**, as a result of water migration through the

5.1 Block of needle ice removed from a frozen soil.

soil towards the zone of freezing. Needle ice gets its name from its vertical structure – it resembles a bundle of needles. Ice lenses are horizontal bodies of ice that form parallel to the ground surface. The thawing of soil ice can result in localised ground saturation and the downslope movement of material, similar to the gelifluction that occurs in the active layer in permafrost regions. These terms will be explained as they are encountered in the sections that follow.

Periglacial Lakeland

Permafrost existed in the Lake District on numerous occasions during the Quaternary period. During the build-up of the glaciers and again during their decay, the areas adjacent to the ice were probably underlain by permafrost. Summits that protruded through the ice as nunataks would also have had permafrost. The last time that permafrost existed in the Lake District was during the restricted and short-lived **Loch Lomond Glaciation**, 13,000–11,500 years ago.

Today, there is no permafrost and no intensive frost activity in the Lake District and therefore truly periglacial conditions are absent. However, although extreme cold is lacking, it generally becomes colder the higher you go on the fells, by about 1ºC per 150 m of ascent. Unfortunately, there is no meteorological station on any Lake District summit and so valuable temperature data by which to characterise the climate are lacking. Some data are available for Scottish and Pennine mountain summits and these indicate that freeze-thaw cycles can occur in any month of the year, but are more common in winter, and that freezing only extends to very shallow depths. Allied to this is the wind regime; British mountains are exposed to strong and persistent winds that restrict the growth of plants at the highest levels and thus augment the role of frost action by keeping some areas of ground bare.

From the climate data that are available, Professor Colin Ballantyne regards British mountain summits as having a **maritime periglacial regime**. This is markedly different from the conditions found in Arctic and Alpine regions, which are significantly colder, but has resulted in the development of some very distinctive small-scale landforms.

In the Lake District we can find two broad categories of periglacial landform. First, there are features associated with former permafrost and/or severe frost activity. Because these features are no longer developing they are called **relict** periglacial landforms. In contrast there are features that are currently forming as a consequence of present-day climatic conditions and these are known as **active** periglacial landforms. This simple sub-division is not always easy to apply in the field because some of the relict features may display evidence for contemporary intermittent activity.

Relict periglacial landforms

The age of the relict periglacial landforms that we can see today in the Lake District is closely linked to their position in the landscape and their relationship to the ice masses that have waxed and waned since about 25,000 years ago. Some, but not all, of the **tors**, **blockfields** and **blockslopes**, **boulder sheets** and **lobes**, and **patterned ground** occur on summits that may have been nunataks during the **Late Devensian Glaciation**, and therefore are likely to have developed between 25,000 and 15,000 years ago adjacent to the upper margin of the Lake District ice-sheet. An alternative explanation is that these features could have formed long before that time and may have been protected from erosion if **cold-based ice** had covered the summits. Nevertheless as the Late Devensian ice melted away, periglacial conditions would have extended into the newly ice-free areas, so some periglacial features would have been created at that time. Re-activation of some of these features is likely to have occurred in association with the severe climate of the ensuing Loch Lomond Glaciation.

Rockfall Talus

Rockfall talus can be defined as an accumulation of angular rock debris below a rock slope. The debris is typically loose and unstable, and tends to shift downslope if walked on. In Britain, scree is the more familiar name for rockfall talus. But whichever term you use, it refers to both the landform and its constituent material.

During and after the disappearance of the glaciers many of the Lake District fells were left with slopes that were steep, craggy and criss-crossed by joints and fractures of various sizes. Because a cold climate still prevailed at that time and there was abundant water from the melting of snow and ice, freeze-thaw action was very effective. As the temperature fell below 0°C, water that had penetrated the rock fissures turned to ice. When water freezes it expands in volume by 9% and if trapped in fissures will exert stress on the surrounding rock that may be sufficient to prise off

5.2 a, Rockfall talus composed of Borrowdale Volcanic Group rock, St. John's in the Vale; b, Rockfall talus composed of Skiddaw Group rock, Scar Crags.

blocks (frost wedging) that then fall and accumulate on the slope below the crag.

Because rockfall talus is abundant in the Lake District (5.2), it has been assumed that freeze-thaw action was a very effective process. However, as was mentioned in Chapter 1, **equifinality** undoubtedly applies with respect to the production of rockfall talus, but for the moment we can continue to treat it under the periglacial heading. Some of the other processes that give rise to slopes of rockfall talus will be dealt with in Chapter 6.

Where hillside crags are relatively straight when seen in plan view, the accompanying talus slopes usually extend across the hillside as a sheet of rock debris and do not vary much in character between one part and another. Where crags are divided by gullies the associated talus slopes may take the form of fans or cones of rock debris spreading out from the base of the gullies. In these cases water flowing down the gullies and snow avalanches have also been involved in shifting the debris.

The sizes of particles on talus slopes can range from small rock fragments of 1–2 cm to boulders several metres in length. It is usual to find the smaller fragments near the top of the talus and for sizes to increase as you go downslope (you'll already know that if you've ever gone up or down a talus slope!). This characteristic is due to **fall sorting**. If a crag sheds rock debris of different sizes, the larger fragments will have greater momentum and on hitting the slope below they bounce or roll and can travel a considerable distance downhill. Conversely, the smaller fragments with less momentum tend to lodge nearer to the base of the crag. Once a talus slope has formed it becomes self-reinforcing as small fragments are easily trapped in the gaps between particles of similar small size near the top, while the larger fragments tend to loose momentum and are trapped only when they encounter similar large-sized particles farther downslope.

The maximum gradient that talus can attain is known as the **angle of repose** – the gradient at which a pile of angular rock fragments can stand without collapsing. Talus slope gradient is something that many fell walkers comment on, especially if they have recently ascended or descended such a slope. Gradients are usually grossly exaggerated with values of 60–70° often stated. In fact, talus slopes rarely exceed 40°. In their upper reaches talus slopes are usually straight and in the 30–40° range; in their lower parts they are normally concave and gradients tend to be 20–30°. So next time you hear someone bragging that they have just run down a 65° scree slope take them to one side, politely disabuse them of their fanciful claim and refer them to this book!

Probably the best-known slopes of rockfall talus in the Lake District are those that rise above Wast Water. They have appeared in countless calendar and picture book photographs, and are also featured in some geomorphological textbooks. However, there is evidence to indicate that processes other than freeze-thaw generated rockfall have been at work on these slopes and this will be explained in Chapter 6. The Wast Water screes may not be of wholly periglacial origin.

It may be the case that many slopes of rockfall talus have developed from a combination of freeze-thaw and other processes – it is not always easy to know which process has contributed most. Nevertheless, talus occurs on virtually all valley sides and also in cirques. If there are crags, there is likely to be talus.

Protalus Ramparts

At the bottom of some talus slopes where the gradient slackens there are vegetation-covered ridges with a scatter of surface boulders. In planform some of these ridges are linear and parallel with the talus base whereas others curve upslope at one or both ends and are therefore arcuate features. They developed as a result of rockfall debris from crags rolling, sliding or bouncing across the surface of a former steeply-inclined snowbed and coming to rest at its foot, as depicted in 5.3. Although the term **protalus rampart** was not coined for these ridges until 1934, both Clifton Ward, in 1873, and John Marr, in 1916, recognised that this mechanism must have previously operated in the Lake District and was responsible for some distinctive talus-foot ridges.

Between 20 and 30 protalus ramparts have been recognised in the Lake District. The origin of a few of these landforms is a matter of dispute so it is not possible to give an exact number. Whether certain talus-foot ridges are protalus ramparts or moraines has proved to be a contentious issue. Protalus ramparts are usually identified on the basis of their proximity to the foot of the talus slope. It has been determined that a true rampart

5.3 Sketch indicating formation of a protalus rampart.

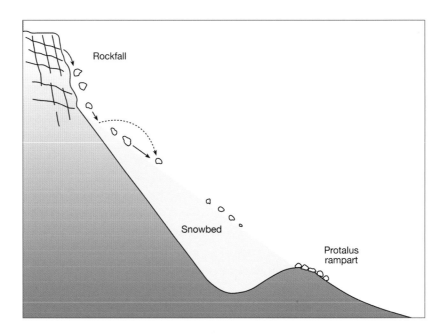

5.4 a, Protalus rampart, in the walled area, below Dead Crags. Compare with Fig 5.3, you will have to imagine the snowbed; b, Closer view of the boulder-strewn Dead Crags rampart.

must be within 70 m of the talus foot. At a greater distance than this the thickness of the snowbed is likely to have been such that it would have been transformed to glacier ice and would have moved outwards and away from the slope, and created a moraine ridge. However even a small glacier can have rockfall debris rolling, sliding and bouncing across its surface. So with some talus-foot ridges it is often difficult to make definitive statements about their origin.

Most of the protalus ramparts in the Lake District occur at sites that were not covered by glacier ice during the Loch Lomond Glaciation. Therefore it has been proposed that they formed during that period of glaciation in locations where snowbeds rather than glaciers developed. Most of these rampart sites face between north and east, on the leeward side of the fells, in positions where snow could accumulate by drifting, and they would have been protected from solar radiation. One of the best protalus ramparts can be seen near Dead Crags on Bakestall (5.4). The track to Skiddaw House passes across the talus slope and the rampart is in the field below. Other examples are to be found along the High Level Route on the northern flanks of Pillar, to the north of Hindscarth Edge, at the foot of the northern slopes of Catstycam, and at the northern end of Goat's Water at the base of the Dow Crag talus. A south-facing rampart is situated on the lower slopes of Herdus, to the west of Great Borne.

A feature that has been considered to be a rampart by some geomorphologists and a **moraine** by others can be seen just east of Newlands Hause, on the Newlands side of the pass where High Hole Beck descends steep slopes below Robinson Crags. The ridge is distinctly arcuate in planform. Assuming Moss Beck can be forded, the ridge is easy to reach being about 150 m from convenient roadside parking. If you have half an hour to spare next time you are going over the pass stop and take a close look. Is it a protalus rampart or is it a moraine?

Tors

Mention of the word **tors** probably conjures up images of Dartmoor, certain Cairngorm summits, or some gritstone edges in the south Pennines. All these areas have their distinctive tors, but tors in the Lake District? Well, actually, yes! Wainwright refers to tors on a number of fells, so they must be there!

Tors are masses of bedrock that rise conspicuously above the surrounding ground surface. They have proved to be more resistant to weathering processes than the adjacent areas either because they consist of harder types of rock or because they possess more widely spaced joints. Therefore they remain higher than the adjoining less resistant areas.

Bedrock knolls created by glacial scouring (Chapter 4) are one type of Lake District tor. Other types owe their morphology to intensive frost wedging during times when periglacial conditions prevailed. These tors comprise angular outcrops encircled or partly obscured by boulders (5.5).

5.5 One of several tors in the Scafell Pike range.

The best examples occur on the highest summits – Bowfell, Esk Pike, Ill Crag, Scafell Pike, Great End and Great Gable. Several of these tors seem to be just great piles of boulders, but bedrock is evident in the middle of them. Others are clearly upstanding bedrock masses surrounded by boulders.

Blockfields and Blockslopes

On the summits and upper slopes of many Lake District fells there are extensive areas of boulders that make for awkward walking if you deviate from established paths. On some routes, like that to Scafell Pike from Esk Hause, you cannot avoid boulders as you cross the shoulders of Ill Crag and Broad Crag and if you want to reach these two tops then more boulders must be negotiated. Wainwright considered it was '…quite impossible to walk with any semblance of dignity…' to the summit of Broad Crag (A. Wainwright 1960, *The Southern Fells*). Geomorphologists refer to such boulder-covered areas as **blockfields** and **blockslopes**. The German word **felsenmeer** is also used for these features.

As with tors, the most impressive blockfields and blockslopes are on fell tops in the Scafell Pike range. They are also present on some lower fells, for example Hart Crag, High Raise, Brandreth, Glaramara and Great Borne.

5.6 a, Blockfield on Broad Crag; b, Blockfield on Great Gable. Note the contrast in sizes and coverage of boulders.

Because the boulders are angular and seemingly arranged in a chaotic manner it is generally considered that they are a product of frost wedging and that the different sizes of boulders on different fells reflect the variations in bedrock joint spacing. This size variation will be evident to those who have traversed Broad Crag, with its large blocks (5.6a), and Great Gable, with its considerably smaller blocks (5.6b). In contrast, Skiddaw Group rocks tend to break down into gravel size fragments so the Skiddaw fells are not noted for abundant boulders.

Equifinality rears its head again with respect to blockfields and block-slopes because they are present in some parts of the world where it is more than likely that they formed as a consequence of deep chemical rotting along bedrock joints rather than by frost wedging. In the Lake District the recency of severe periglacial activity strongly suggests a frost-related origin for these features.

Boulder Sheets and Lobes

Where concentrations of boulders occur on moderately steep hillsides they are generally disposed as sheet-like features that extend for tens if not hundreds of metres across-slope and downslope (5.7a). These boulder-strewn areas are usually terminated at their downslope margin by a long low bank or riser, and give many fellsides a marked stepped appearance. The riser may extend across slope at a consistent elevation but where there are local increases in hillside gradient the riser becomes more irregular or crenellate in planform and conspicuous boulder lobes may be evident (5.7b). Lobes are areas that exhibit distinct bulging and they can be very impressive features with risers up to 3–4 m high. The existence of a prominent riser indicates that the boulders have moved some distance downslope from the places they were produced by frost wedging and have overridden boulders farther downslope.

The process that caused the boulders to travel downslope is **solifluction** – the slow downslope movement of hillside debris in association with freezing and thawing. There are two parts to the process – frost creep and gelifluction. The former involves the repeated lifting (frost heave) and resettlement of debris as soil ice develops and then thaws; on slopes gravity also influences the resettlement of debris and so it gradually moves downhill. The latter is the sliding or flowing of saturated debris as a result of the surface layers thawing while the subsurface remains frozen. It is not entirely clear if frost creep and gelifluction were of equal importance in boulder movement; the issue continues to be debated.

Boulder sheets and lobes are especially well developed on the west-facing slope of Scafell – to make their acquaintance take a direct line from Burnmoor Tarn to the summit ridge. They can also be found on Carrock Fell (5.7a), Great End (5.7b), Kirk Fell, Brandreth, and many other fells.

There is a notable absence of boulder sheets and lobes on fells under-lain by Skiddaw Group rocks because, as mentioned earlier, when these rocks break down they usually produce fragments that are smaller than boulder size. Nevertheless, solifluction sheets and lobes of a different

5.7 a, Boulder sheet on Carrock Fell; b, The steep riser (frontal slope) of a boulder lobe on Great End; c, Vegetated lobe on Skiddaw. The survey pole divisions are 20 cm.

kind can be found and are particularly clear on the northern slopes of Skiddaw at a height of 700–800 m adjacent to the fence that runs out to Bakestall. These sheets and lobes are smaller than their counterparts on the Borrowdale Volcanic fells, are generally covered by vegetation, and the risers rarely exceed 1 m in height (5.7c). Where the vegetation cover is incomplete the composition of the debris can be seen to be predominantly gravel size fragments within a silty soil.

Patterned Ground

Patterned ground is the name applied to the regular and irregular ground surface patterns that are commonly encountered in periglacial areas. These landforms may be characterised by alternations of coarse and fine debris, by microrelief, or by the nature and extent of the vegetation. Surface patterns can occur as either sorted or nonsorted forms. In sorted patterned ground coarse debris is clearly separated from fine debris; in nonsorted patterned ground it is microrelief (mounds, depressions, ridges, furrows), the vegetation cover (the juxtaposition of vegetated and unvegetated ground), or both that give rise to patterning.

The geometry of patterned ground changes in accordance with slope gradient. On flat surfaces and slopes with a gradient of less than about 5° sorted patterns consist of circular or polygonal structures. As gradient increases these features become increasingly elongated and eventually grade into stripe patterns. Nonsorted patterns generally show a transition from hummocky terrain on flat surfaces to relief stripes on slopes.

Relict patterned ground is not very common in the Lake District but sorted patterns can be seen in several places amongst the blockfields on the Scafell to Great End ridge. The best example I know of is on Ill Crag and consists of circles of boulders about 2 m in diameter with centres that are covered by vegetation (5.8a). Some boulders are present beneath the vegetation but most of the debris in the centres is of smaller size, which explains why plants have been able to colonise these areas.

There has been a great deal of debate and expenditure of energy regarding the processes that create sorted patterned ground and it is still not clear exactly how these features develop. Sorted patterns of similar and greater dimensions to the Lake District examples are widespread in permafrost areas and, by analogy, a permafrost-related origin probably applies here as well. But just how and why does debris become sorted by size and produce circular patterns?

Several reasons have been advanced to explain sorted patterns. The sorting process, whereby coarse and fine debris have come to occupy different areas, is attributed to the upward and outward movement of boulders as a result of frost heave and frost creep. The process that controls the regularity of the patterns is thought to be one of convective circulation in the debris. During thawing of the active layer, density variations are established in the soil and/or water. Soil density variations and water temperature variations generate buoyancy forces and these, in turn, lead to convective motion in the soil and water. Many geomorphologists consider convection to be the driving force for sorted patterned ground.

Nonsorted patterned ground is also quite rare in the Lake District but a good place to observe relief stripes (vegetation covered ridges and furrows) is in the col between Skiddaw and Skiddaw Little Man at 800 m. The stripes trend northwest – southeast across the col, on the west side of the fence (5.8b). The ridge crests are about 50 cm apart and in places the vegetation mat has been ruptured revealing a dark grey stony soil, which makes the ridges even more prominent. An unusual aspect of these stripes is that they retain the same morphology irrespective of the change in gradient between the slopes leading into the col and the flat floor of the col.

The origin of relief stripes is as enigmatic as the origin of sorted patterns, if not more so. One idea relates them to greater amounts of frost heave along lines where subsurface water percolation was concentrated. That may be valid on slopes but is unlikely to apply on the floor of the

5.8 Relict patterned ground: a, A sorted circle, Scafell Pike range; b, Nonsorted relief stripes in the col between Skiddaw and Skiddaw Little Man. The survey pole divisions are 20 cm.

Skiddaw col. These features clearly require more investigation in order to explain how they developed.

It was mentioned earlier that some relict periglacial features may display evidence for contemporary intermittent activity. The ruptured vegetation mat on parts of the Skiddaw relief stripes could be due to contemporary frost activity, to wind (the col certainly funnels the wind), or both. This is another aspect worthy of investigation.

Active periglacial landforms

In the 1870s Clifton Ward recognised active patterned ground in parts of the northern Lake District but he thought that heavy rain was responsible for its formation. Since then active periglacial features have been recorded on many fells and numerous reports describing their morphology and discussing their formative processes have been published in the scientific literature. Contemporary frost action is responsible for these features, but variations in rock type, altitude, vegetation cover, aspect and gradient also control which forms develop and where they can develop. Present-day frost action is nowhere near as powerful a force as it was when the last glaciers existed and does not give rise to particularly bold landscape features. Nevertheless, it is responsible for some fascinating small-scale forms. Once you 'get your eye in' you will begin to identify and appreciate the role that frost plays.

Frost-Heaved Ground

Ground at all altitudes is susceptible to frost heave and the effects can best be appreciated in areas with silty soils containing a moderate quantity of stones. When the temperature falls to 0°C and below, water in the subsoil is drawn towards the ground surface. The water freezes just below the surface and forms needle ice (5.1). As the ice crystals grow they lift the ground surface by a small amount. Some stones may be too large for needle ice to lift so 'holes' form above them or gaps open around them (5.9a). Walking on a footpath in which needle ice is present causes your feet to sink slightly as your weight crushes the ice. If you look at your footsteps you will see the needle ice and the thin layer of soil particles it has lifted, as shown in 5.9b.

The effects produced by needle ice on footpaths and elsewhere are interesting phenomena rather than types of landforms. Apart from its

5.9 a, A frost-heaved footpath; b, Needle ice in a footpath. The scale bar divisions are 5 cm.

ability to heave the surface, needle ice also breaks up the surface by loosening material. In this way it is preparing the surface for further erosion. During periods of heavy rainfall, water may find it easier to carry away material from paths that have undergone repeated episodes of frost heave. If left unchecked this can lead to serious erosion and gully development over a period of years. Walkers are not necessarily responsible for all of the footpath erosion in the Lake District.

Debris Sheets and Lobes

Solifluction occurs today on the Lakeland fells, but not with the same intensity as was required to move boulders downslope and create the pronounced boulder sheets and lobes described and illustrated earlier. Present-day solifluction affects stony soils and produces sheets and lobes composed of such debris. Morphologically these features are similar to their bouldery counterparts in that they are terminated at their downslope margin by a low bank or riser that may extend for some distance across slope at a consistent elevation or have a crenellate planform. Generally the risers are less than 1 m in height; sometimes they are just a few centimetres high. Irrespective of size the risers invariably form a small wall of vegetation holding back an area of stony soil and for this reason they are sometimes referred to as turf-banked sheets and lobes (5.10).

Debris sheets and lobes can be seen on the west-facing slopes of Helvellyn, on the northern slopes of Skiddaw and Blencathra, and on

5.10 Active debris lobes on Helvellyn. The survey pole divisions are 20 cm.

Hindscarth and Robinson. In each case you will have to ascend to above 600 m in order to see them.

On Skiddaw active debris sheets and lobes occur in the same area as the relict sheets and lobes depicted in 5.7c. The distinction between these types is based entirely on appearance: the former have stony soil exposed on their treads and have vegetated risers while the latter are completely covered with vegetation. It is possible that the relict sheets and lobes are intermittently active. This might be tested by careful measurement of rates of movement but would require accurate surveying over several winter seasons.

Patterned Ground

Probably the most distinctive type of active periglacial landform in the Lake District is **patterned ground**. Clifton Ward noted the '…strange appearance upon many of the fell-tops, or sides, as if stones had been sown along regular lines close together'. Active sorted patterned ground has since been recorded above 600 m on many fells, with Skiddaw, Blencathra, the Grasmoor group and the Helvellyn ridge having extensive areas.

5.11 Active patterned ground: a, A sorted circle near Cold Pike. The scale bar divisions are 5 cm; b, Sorted stripes on Skiddaw. The survey pole divisions are 20 cm.

As with the relict sorted patterns described earlier, the active forms are characterised by the clear separation of coarse and fine debris, and the geometry of the patterns changes as slope gradient changes. On flat surfaces and slopes of less than about 5°, sorted patterns consist of circular or polygonal structures (5.11a). These features become increasingly elongated and eventually grade into stripe patterns as gradient increases (5.11b). Active sorted patterns are of considerably smaller dimensions than relict patterns and consist of smaller rock fragments; circles and polygons do not normally exceed 30–40 cm in diameter, and stripe widths are usually less than 50 cm.

Circular and polygonal patterns are less common than stripes but in each type of pattern the coarser fragments occupy shallow troughs and the finer particles are slightly elevated above the troughs. This relationship is best seen in winter when the ground freezes; in summer the distinction is less clear because the actions of wind, rain and animals (including passing walkers) tend to destroy the patterns. However, the patterns reform with the next winter frosts.

Excavations into sorted patterns during periods of freezing have revealed ice lenses within the finer debris of some patterns and needle ice within others. This suggests that frost heave and frost creep play some part in the separation of coarser from finer fragments, and it is frost heave that lifts the finer debris slightly higher than the coarser debris. Again, as with relict sorted patterns, the regularity of the features is attributed to buoyancy forces and convective circulation induced by variations in soil density and/or water temperature during thawing.

Sorted patterned ground is a fascinating phenomenon. I can guarantee that once you have recognised it you will not forget it and will start looking for it on all your high level winter walks.

Ploughing Boulders

Ploughing boulders are surface boulders that move downslope faster than the soil in which they are embedded; in so doing they push soil and vegetation into a mound on their downslope side and leave a linear depression or furrow on their upslope side, revealing their direction of movement (5.12). In some instances low ridges of soil have also been pushed up by boulder movement and flank the depression. The first description of such boulders in the Lake District was by Thomas Hay in the 1930s. He called them 'gliders' or 'gliding blocks' but the term ploughing boulders has since taken precedence.

They can be found on many fell sides above about 450 m. Some excellent examples can be seen on the western slopes of Dollywaggon Pike, just below the path to Helvellyn, and on the slopes of Grey Friar, Swirl How and Great Carrs that converge on Fairfield Hause. I have also seen them on Blencathra, Bowscale Fell, Bannerdale Crags, Seat Sandal, Raise, and between the eastern top of Stybarrow Dodd and Glencoyne Head. In fact, many boulders on grass-covered fell sides will show some degree

5.12 A ploughing boulder on Dollywaggon Pike. The scale bar divisions are 5 cm.

of ploughing activity, and I have noted them on moraines at elevations considerably below 450 m.

Ploughing boulders are one manifestation of contemporary solifluction, and in particular gelifluction. The boulders are undergoing slow downslope movement because they have a greater degree of thermal conductivity than the surrounding soil. As the ground freezes, the freezing plane is able to pass through boulders more rapidly and this results in soil water being drawn towards the base of the boulder where it freezes and forms an ice lens. Shallow excavations alongside frozen ploughing boulders in the Scottish Highlands have revealed ice lenses up to 3 cm thick.

When thawing sets in, the greater thermal conductivity of the boulders causes the ice lenses to melt before the ground in front of the boulders has had time to thaw. As a consequence the soil below the boulders is saturated and the water has nowhere to go. When the ground in front of the boulders thaws the trapped water escapes and the boulders slip forward a little. By this mechanism boulders move slowly downslope and push the soil in front of them into a mound.

The rate at which ploughing boulders move in the Lake District is unknown but some measurements are available for boulders on the Moor House Nature Reserve in the northern Pennines and on several Scottish mountains. These measurements reveal that boulders can move downslope by up to 6–7 cm per year. However, this does not mean that all boulders move at the same rate, indeed in some mild winters boulders may not move at all. The rate of movement is also related to slope gradient, boulder size, soil characteristics, number of freeze-thaw cycles and, after ploughing their way downslope for many years, some boulders may have come to a halt because they are no longer able to overcome the resistance of a large mound of ploughed-up soil. The furrows behind some ploughing boulders are 5–10 m long but it is not known over what period boulders have moved those distances.

Tailpiece

Whereas glaciers created some large-scale landforms of erosion and deposition in the Lake District, the role of periglacial processes has been to modify the surfaces and produce landforms of much more modest dimensions. Nevertheless a rich variety of relict landforms is present and active features indicate that freezing and thawing continues to affect the area, albeit on a rather restricted scale.

In recent decades Lake District winters have become somewhat milder and wetter. At certain times temperature may still fall to below freezing at all levels, but the current warming trend may eventually put an end to that. As the frequency of frost activity declines so the prominence of active periglacial features on the Lake District fells will also decline and the distinctive patterns that characterise many slopes of gravel-size fragments will be no more. You had better go now and become familiar with these features before we lose them completely.

CHAPTER SIX

Hillslope processes and landforms

Introduction

VIRTUALLY THE ENTIRE LAKE DISTRICT consists of slopes. Whether it is steep, moderate or gentle, sloping terrain is almost everywhere. As every hill walker knows, there is not a lot of flat ground once you start going up. Most of the landforms considered in this book are located on slopes or are made up of areas of sloping ground. The glacial and periglacial features described in Chapters 4 and 5 are prime examples of this, as are many of the landforms that are dealt with in Chapters 7, 8 and 9. In fact, the Lake District owes its slopes to geological forces and **glacial**, **periglacial** and **fluvial** (river) processes.

The most spectacular slopes are probably those topped by great rock buttresses and with screes sweeping down to the valley floor, as can be seen alongside Wast Water or on the Napes face of Great Gable. Almost as impressive are the long, long slopes of low, broken crag interspersed with seemingly smooth, vegetated areas that characterise the sidewalls of many glacial troughs. Wainwright did not hesitate to let us know what he thought of having to ascend certain slopes. Of the route from Mickleden to Pike o'Stickle via the south scree, 'In a buttoned-up plastic mac, the ascent is purgatory.' (A. Wainwright 1958, *The Central Fells*), and of the direct ascent of Kirk Fell from Wasdale Head, '... a relentless and unremitting treadmill, a turf-clutching crawl, not a walk.' (A. Wainwright 1966, *The Western Fells*). It seems he didn't appreciate some of the steeper hillsides.

The very existence of sloping ground allows another important geomorphological control to play a role in shaping the surface and creating some distinctive features. That control is gravity. Slope materials, be they rock or sediment, have a tendency to undergo movement downhill because of gravity. Sometimes water and ice can assist gravity by reducing the strength of slope materials and preparing them for gravitational transport. Taken together, the processes by which materials travel from higher to lower slope positions are called **mass movements** and because the landsurface is being gradually lowered by them the term **mass wasting** is applied to such activity. A more familiar and frequently used term is **landslide**, but when slope materials move they do not always slide; they can fall, topple, flow or creep, and may produce a variety of features. Mass movements are very diverse in their style and rate of movement. Generally speaking, materials on long steep slopes tend to travel greater distances if they are disturbed, but there are many examples where, for one or more reasons, this has not been the case.

There is abundant evidence to show that Lake District slopes have undergone marked changes since the last glaciers disappeared. Rock and sediment have been, and still are being, disturbed and moved downslope. The scars of such movements and the masses of displaced material below are to be seen in many places, although some are more obvious than others. Once you have recognised the different types of evidence for past and present slope instability you will quickly realise that there are few slopes that have escaped from some form of mass movement.

The factors controlling mass movements include the geological characteristics of the slope materials, the water content of these materials, and the slope gradient. External factors such as human actions and earth tremors can also be hugely influential. Understanding why and how slopes change through time is more than of passing interest to geomorphologists and hill walkers. It is also of great practical value because it can inform us about the potential hazards associated with construction projects. During excavation work for buildings, roads, reservoirs, and upland drainage schemes, slope materials may be destabilised or new slopes created. The result is that mass movements may be triggered, sometimes with disastrous consequences.

Before getting on to the different features produced by mass movements, the term **paraglacial** needs to be introduced and defined because it is increasingly being invoked to explain some slope landforms that occur in upland areas like the Lake District. When glaciers retreat they leave behind a landscape that is unstable and vulnerable to further change. The steep rock walls of glacial troughs lose the support previously provided by the ice and can shed large quantities of rock either as discrete **rockfalls** or large-scale **rock-slope failures**. Similarly, the accumulations of glacial sediment are also modified, principally by running water and snow avalanches. These processes can continue to affect the landscape long after the glaciers have gone. The term **paraglacial** was introduced in recognition of the fact that glaciation provided the impetus for these subsequent changes.

Mass movements can be categorised with respect to the type of material involved in gravitational transport. There are those that occur in bedrock on the steeper hillsides and those that are restricted to the layers of peat and glacial sediments that cover the bedrock on less steep slopes.

Mass movements in bedrock

On steep mountain slopes mass movements in bedrock take several forms (6.1) and are usually regarded as **paraglacial** landforms. However, other processes can also lead to the downslope movement of large rock masses: primarily earth tremors, high water pressures in rock joints, and the progressive weakening of bedrock as a result of chemical weathering along joints. Because these mass movements most likely occurred several thousands of years ago it is virtually impossible to know under what circumstances they developed. It is also difficult to know if these mass movements occurred as single events or whether the landforms we see today are the result of several phases of movement.

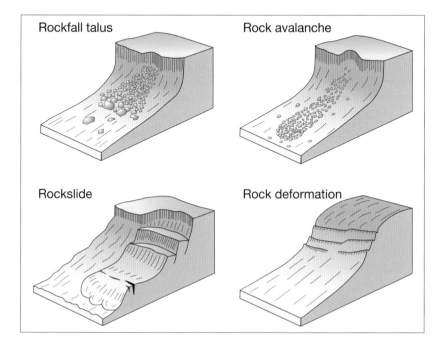

6.1 Types of mass movements in bedrock.

Although 6.1 shows four discrete types of mass movement, on some fellsides more complex forms have occurred. For example, part of a slope may have undergone some degree of deformation while a neighbouring part may have undergone sliding, and some of the sliding rock masses may have disintegrated to produce a talus of large boulders. Irrespective of the type, mass movements in bedrock contribute to the widening of valleys and the enlargement of cirques. They provide debris that the next glaciers can incorporate and carry away. Because there have been many glacial and interglacial phases, mass movements in bedrock have probably been a significant factor in shaping the Lake District.

Rockfall Talus

Rockfall talus was dealt with in Chapter 5: *Periglacial processes and landforms*, and was attributed to **frost wedging**. Whilst this process may account for much of the hillside talus, it is unlikely to explain all occurrences.

There are quite a number of places in the Lake District where talus consists of many very large boulders and in these cases it seems likely that it is the result of mass movement rather than periglacial activity. While it is reasonable to infer that the removal of ice support led to the collapse and disintegration of large sections of crags and resulted in spreads of enormous boulders, rockfalls associated with earth tremors are also known to have occurred in more recent times. In August 1786 a tremor, centred on Whitehaven, dislodged rock on Pillar, Helvellyn and Red Pike (Buttermere). A tremor in July 1787 caused another rockfall on Helvellyn, and the Carlisle tremor on Boxing Day 1979 brought down rock from Kern Knotts on Great Gable. Those who tackle the Gable Traverse path must cross the debris of this rockfall. We cannot possibly know the true extent of rockfalls associated with earth tremors in the more distant past.

The Bowder Stone in Borrowdale (6.2) is one of the largest boulders in the Lake District and detailed investigation has demonstrated that it is a product of rockfall, rather than a glacial **erratic** as some people have suggested. Unfortunately the Bowder Stone tends to be thought of in isolation, but if you visit it I recommend that you also clamber a short way up the adjacent wooded hillside where you will see many other massive boulders. Although these are somewhat smaller than the Bowder Stone they are, nevertheless, still of impressive dimensions, and are testimony to the magnitude of the crag collapse from which they derive.

Some other places with clusters of immense boulders resulting from

6.2 The Bowder Stone in Borrowdale.

crag collapse are Dove Crag in Dovedale (6.3), Raven Crag in the valley of Pasture Beck, Moss Crag in Glencoyne Wood, Auterstone Crag on Arthur's Pike, Carrock Fell End, Deer Bield Crag in Far Easedale, Sampson's Stones in upper Eskdale, and Erin Crag in the valley of Red Dell Beck in the Coniston fells. One thing to remember about all these examples is that when the crags disintegrated the boulders were probably even bigger than they are now; impact with other boulders and the ground surface reduced them in size.

At a number of places along the foot of the Wast Water screes there are boulders that are substantially larger than those to be seen elsewhere along that rough lakeshore path (6.4a). On top of the crags above these boulders the ground surface consists of a series of low, grass-covered ridges and shallow depressions that run parallel with the edge of the crags for 150–300 m (6.4b). The ridges are huge slices of rock and the depressions between them are tension cracks. These areas of 'corrugated' terrain are remnants of major crag collapses. How much of the hillside overlooking Wast Water disintegrated in this manner is simply unknown and most of

6.3 This spread of large boulders below Dove Crag in Dovedale is the product of a crag collapse.

6.4 a, The Wast Water screes, large boulders are present just above the water line; b, Grassy ridges and depressions on the cliff top above the Wast Water screes. Wainwright thought (incorrectly) that this unusual terrain was associated with a bed of limestone.

a

b

the rock that fell is probably below the water line. The boulders that have to be negotiated when following the lakeshore path may actually be some of the smaller-sized debris that did not descend below lake level. We can only speculate about the size of boulders that rest beneath the water.

Wainwright recorded the unusual ground surface form shown in 6.4b in his depiction of the ridge route from Illgill Head to Whin Rigg but thought it was due to sinks and potholes in a bed of limestone. On this occasion he was wrong.

Rock Avalanche Boulder Tongues

The catastrophic collapse and disintegration of a hillside crag can result in the falling debris being propelled a considerable distance downslope as a **rock avalanche**. When the debris eventually comes to rest it forms a tongue-like pile of boulders that stands above the level of the adjacent ground surface. Such landforms are common in many of the high mountain ranges of the world; they can extend down valley for several kilometres and can involve millions of tonnes of rock.

Only one rock avalanche boulder tongue has been identified in the Lake District – in Burtness Comb overlooking Buttermere. This feature was previously regarded as moraine but detailed investigation revealed characteristics that were inconsistent with a glacial origin. Rather, the location of the feature within the Comb, its plan-form morphology, and the nature of the constituent debris indicate it is the result of a rock avalanche. The boulder tongue is 700 m in length and exceeds 100 m in width. Its average thickness is about 5 m and the volume of rock debris is estimated to be 300,000 m^3. These values are rather low in comparison to rock avalanche boulder tongues elsewhere in the world, but in a Lake District context it is a significant and an imposing landform.

The margins of the boulder tongue are clearly defined and stand several metres above the surrounding ground. Low, sinuous ridges and hummocks occur on the surface of the tongue. In parts there is a cover of vegetation but the abundance of boulders is evident. The source of the rock debris was Grey Crag on the flanks of High Stile. It is not known when the boulder tongue formed but differences in the degree of boulder weathering between the upper and lower parts of the tongue have been detected through measurements of boulder hardness; this suggests that two rock avalanches are likely to have occurred. The lower part of the boulder tongue represents the first phase of avalanching, the upper part the second phase (6.5).

6.5 The upper part of the Burtness Comb rock avalanche boulder tongue extending from upper left to lower right.

Rock avalanches are major hazards in mountain ranges with rapidly shrinking glaciers and/or frequent earth tremors. They must be spectacular events, but very few have been witnessed. The rock avalanche boulder tongue in Burtness Comb tells of a dramatic chapter in the shaping of the mountain; there must have been quite a noise and clouds of dust as Grey Crag collapsed and sent masses of boulders hurtling down the Comb.

Rockslides

On some fellsides there are extensive areas of ground that have moved a short distance downslope by sliding along a plane of structural weakness (a **shear plane**) in the rock. The slipped rock masses have tended to remain largely intact and are now lodged lower on the slope. Such **rockslides** usually have a distinct **headscarp** – a cliff or crag up to few tens of metres in height from which the rock slid away. In some instances a certain amount of rock disintegration took place as sliding occurred and resulted in numerous boulders, rock pinnacles and deep clefts.

Several big rockslides are present in the Lake District and have created some very prominent features that many walkers will be familiar with even though they may not have realised how they formed. Wainwright illustrated four rockslides in his Pictorial Guides: first, the summit ridge of Helm Crag with its much photographed and popularised rock formations (1.3); second, Dovenest Crag in Comb Gill (Rosthwaite Fell); third, Hackney Holes and Littledale Edge (Robinson); fourth, Revelin Crag (Crag Fell) (6.6a). He thought Helm Crag and Dovenest Crag were the result of a 'natural convulsion' – and he was right, but he makes no comment about the origin of the features on Robinson and Crag Fell.

According to the British Geological Survey the rockslide that created Hackney Holes and the broadly stepped terrain on the south side of Littledale Edge is the largest such feature in the Lake District. Their map shows the rockslide covering most of the fellside from the ridge crest to Gatesgarthdale Beck, an area of 1.7 km².

Several other sizeable rockslides exist in Lakeland; some are away from popular paths and are therefore largely unknown, for example Rough Edge on Caudale Moor (6.6b) and Cotley on Black Combe, others are adjacent to or are traversed by paths. One of the largest in the latter category occupies the fellside between Grisedale Tarn and Deepdale Hause. It is crossed by thousands of walkers each year but was not recorded by either Wainwright or the Geological Survey. To the east of Grisedale Beck, the

6.6 a, One of the most spectacular rockslides in the Lake District occupies ground on the north side of Crag Fell above the foot of Ennerdale Water. Wainwright drew attention to certain features on this slope; b, The rockslide at Rough Edge above the Kirkstone Pass.

footpath to Deepdale Hause first crosses boggy ground and then rises to enter an area consisting of many narrow ridges and depressions. Some ridges have crests of shattered rock, some depressions are boulder strewn. This terrain continues all the way to the hause. The area of rocksliding can be traced for over a kilometre along the fellside and up to a height of 850 m, just below the summit of Fairfield.

Rock Deformations

At certain times in the past some fellsides were deformed by the slow mass movement of rock – a process known as **rock mass creep** or **gravitational spreading**. **Rock deformations** are usually less pronounced than the other types of movement in bedrock because the rock has travelled only a short distance and has not undergone much, if any, disintegration. Deformation can occur as a result of either **extensional** or **compressional** forces acting on the rock. The former tend to act on the upper parts of hillslopes and, as a result, the rock body separates into slices from a few metres to tens of metres in width; these slices gradually move downslope. The latter forces are more common farther downslope and lead to the bulging of hillsides and upthrust ridges. Irrespective of the type of deformation, it can embrace large areas and results in low ridges and depressions that may extend for several hundreds of metres across slopes.

6.7 a, Antiscarps and depressions resulting from rock deformation near Hausewell Brow on the northern slopes of Clough Head; b, Part of the longest and most distinctive antiscarp near the summit of Kirk Fell; one of Wainwright's 'natural dykes'.

In most Lake District examples the ridges do not exceed 5 m in height and in cross-section they are asymmetric with their steeper side facing upslope. Such ridges are known as **antiscarps**. Several antiscarps occur above Hausewell Brow on the Old Coach Road between St. John's in the Vale and Matterdale (6.7a), and close to the summit of Kirk Fell another quite impressive set of 15 antiscarps can be seen. Clifton Ward described a series of 'linear depressions or trenches' on Kirk Fell in an article published in 1873 and Wainwright noted 'natural dykes' near the summit on the ascent from Wasdale Head (A. Wainwright 1966, *The Western Fells*). The longest and most distinctive of the Kirk Fell antiscarps and depressions runs from just south of the summit towards the northwest for 600 m (6.7b) and can be picked out by the contour crenellations on the 1:25,000 scale OS map. In one place the crest of the antiscarp stands 8 m above the depression.

Because rock deformations are not quite as prominent in the landscape as other forms of mass movement in bedrock it is likely that many more remain to be discovered, probably on those fellsides that are little visited and therefore largely unknown.

Mass movements in superficial materials

Superficial materials are those that cover the bedrock and for the most part they consist of glacial sediments that are, in turn, overlain by peat. Where the gradient is less than about 10° these materials can be several metres thick; on steeper gradients of 20–30° they tend to be much thinner. It is on the steeper slopes with thinner materials that the majority of mass movements in superficial materials occur. Nevertheless, some spectacular features can result.

Debris Slides

The characteristic mass movement in superficial materials is the **debris slide**. Although regarded as a gravitational feature, sliding often occurs during or following periods of prolonged and heavy rainfall that serve to saturate the materials and to reduce friction between the particles. Sliding can also occur as a consequence of weathering and soil formation in the upper part of the glacial sediments. Again, the friction between particles is lowered and a plane of weakness is established between the weathered material and the less weathered material below. In many cases it has been noted that the sliding surface is associated with the development of a compact soil **iron pan**. During intense rain this can act as a barrier to the percolation of water and, as a result, a mass of material begins to slide and eventually comes to rest some distance downslope.

6.8 shows the attributes of a debris slide. At the head of a slide there is usually an arcuate scarp that reveals the nature of the slope materials and the thickness that has moved away. Downslope of this scarp is the surface along which sliding occurred and on which there are large blocks of material, still upright as shown by their vegetation, but clearly no longer in their original position. Farther downslope is the zone of debris deposition. This is usually a chaotic mass of vegetated blocks, inclined at various angles, and debris slurry with large stones. The margin of debris deposition is usually very sharp and the downslope limit normally coincides with a marked reduction in slope gradient.

Debris slides occur each year in Lakeland. Most are well away from popular paths but sometimes they bury or destroy paths. Some debris slides enter streams and may cause a temporary blockage. 6.9a shows a slide that crossed the line of the Old Coach Road beneath White Pike in August 2004, whereas the slide in 6.9b dumped its debris into Raise Beck, between Seat Sandal and Dollywaggon Pike, in the spring of 2008.

Vegetation can quickly colonise the surface of a debris slide and within a few years a site can become almost unrecognisable and is easily passed without being noticed. Next time you see a fresh debris slide keep it in mind and remember to check it out when you pass that way again. You'll be surprised just how quickly it blends back into its surroundings.

6.8 Sketch showing the attributes and form of a debris slide.

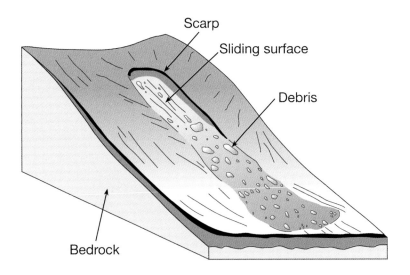

LAKE DISTRICT MOUNTAIN LANDFORMS

If all the superficial materials on a slope are removed by debris sliding, the exposed rock surface is worthy of detailed inspection – you might be lucky and find **striations** left by the last glaciers.

6.9 a, This debris slide destroyed part of the Old Coach Road below White Pike in August 2004; b, A debris slide from May 2008 in the upper part of the Raise Beck valley.

Other hillslope landforms

Terracettes

On some moderately steep grassy hillsides, small closely and regularly spaced step-like features that extend for tens of metres parallel to the contours may be seen. They form a broad staircase of narrow pathways with vegetation-covered risers and, usually, bare treads, and have been likened to tiers of seats in a theatre or sports arena (6.10).

Opinion concerning the origin of **terracettes** is divided between those geomorphologists who favour their formation as a result of grazing animals traversing the hillside and those who view them as a consequence of a mass movement process.

Terracettes may develop within several weeks of sheep and cattle being allowed to graze on some hillslopes. In such cases there can be no doubt that the animals are responsible. Elsewhere terracettes are present on slopes that are not grazed. In some of these examples the terracettes occur on hillsides that have been undercut by streams or on the sides of gullies, suggesting perhaps that they formed in response to the larger-scale removal of soil and sediment.

6.10 Terracettes on the side of a moraine.

In the absence of animals terracettes have been attributed to either a small-scale sliding or creeping process. Sliding requires the existence of a plane of weakness in the soil in order to facilitate movement, and usually occurs quite quickly; on the other hand creeping is a barely perceptible form of mass movement in which the soil migrates downslope over a long time. From observations and analyses of soils it has been claimed that both mechanisms are capable of producing terracettes. If that is so, then they are yet another example of **equifinality**.

In the Lake District terracettes are present on many hillsides, and given that sheep are ubiquitous the likelihood of their involvement in terracette formation cannot be ignored.

Sheep Scars

If there is a question about the role of sheep in terracette formation, there can be no such doubt about how **sheep scars** develop. Sheep are not quite as stupid as they are often made out to be and in response to their need for a bit of protection and comfort, on what are otherwise exposed hillsides, they sometimes create linear or arcuate breaks in the vegetation and soil (6.11a).

In adverse conditions sheep select places on slopes that provide them with some shelter. Repeated use of these sites destroys the vegetation and exposes the soil. As the sheep snuggle down they trample the bare soil

6.11 a, Sheep scar (with a sheep rubbing its backside) on Latrigg b, Close view of sheep scar showing wool caught in the exposed roots.

and rub against the upslope edge of the emerging scar. This loosens the soil which may then be kicked or washed across the grassy area immediately downslope.

Over time a distinct scar forms, and on some hillslopes they are abundant. Close inspection of the scars will show wool caught in the exposed roots (6.11b) and much dung – evidence, if it were needed, that sheep are the culprits.

Tailpiece

That mass movement processes have had a significant influence on the Lake District landscape is beyond question. Since the last glaciers decayed in the high comb(e)s and valley heads, the fellsides have not remained static and unchanged; rather, they have been very dynamic components of the landscape. Although large-scale mass movements in bedrock are no longer common, substantial rockfalls do occur occasionally – as happened at Deer Bield Crag in Far Easedale in 1979 (see 1.5). Of greater frequency are debris slides, and we may anticipate that they will increase in number in the coming years if predictions concerning climate change and an associated upwards trend in rainfall prove to be correct. These will create additional problems for those who live and work in the National Park and, on a small-scale, will modify the form of the fellsides.

CHAPTER SEVEN

Rivers, Lakes and Tarns

Introduction

I N H I S P O E M *The Rime of the Ancient Mariner*, Coleridge penned the words 'Water, water everywhere'. Although the story was inspired by exploratory ocean voyages to the ends of the Earth, those immortal words could also apply to the Lake District, because on occasions it does seem that water is everywhere. But if it were not for water the area would need a different name!

The rivers, lakes and tarns owe their existence to glaciation and precipitation. Glacial ice carved out the basins in which the lakes and tarns are found, and precipitation provides the water that keeps them filled via the streams and rivers.

Rain is the major component of precipitation (the rest is made up of snow, sleet and hail) and the Lake District does receive rather a lot. Several eminent writers have referred to the character of Lakeland rain. Wordsworth, in his *Guide to the Lakes*, wrote 'The rain here comes down heartily…', which is perhaps something of an understatement. In contrast, Hugh Walpole in *Rogue Herries* was rather more forthcoming – 'This rain was the especial and peculiar property of the district …. rain of a relentless, determined, soaking, penetrating kind. No other rain anywhere, at least in the British Isles (which have a prerogative of many sorts of rain), falls with so determined a fanatical obstinacy as does this rain.' *Wet Weather* was the title of a chapter in Harry Griffin's first book, *Inside the Real Lakeland*. As well as discussing this aspect of the Lakeland climate he also had the good sense to advise visitors on what to do on rainy days. However, as far as I can see most of his suggestions involved getting wet!

Amounts of precipitation vary enormously from place to place in the Lake District. For example, Seathwaite in Borrowdale (7.1), the wettest habitation in England, receives about 3400 mm per year. On 18th–19th

RIVERS, LAKES AND TARNS   • 127 •

7.1 Seathwaite in Borrowdale, the wettest inhabited place in England.

November 2009, 314 mm of rain was recorded at Seathwaite making this the wettest 24-hour period in England since records began. Farther down the valley at Rosthwaite the annual amount is 2550 mm, at Grange 2300 mm, and at Keswick 1500 mm. Therefore Keswick receives less than one half of the amount that falls at Seathwaite, yet it is only 12 km distant. Furthermore, the head of Borrowdale figures in two British weather records: the accolade for highest precipitation in one year is held by the Sprinkling Tarn rain gauge which recorded 6527 mm in 1954, and the highest average annual precipitation (i.e. the wettest place) is Styhead Tarn with 4391 mm (7.2). How do these values compare with that where you live?

The reason why the Lake District receives these quantities of precipitation is because of the influence the fells have on the predominantly westerly airflow. The moist Atlantic air is forced to rise over the fells causing it to cool, the moisture condenses and precipitation results. Amounts of precipitation are greatest in the high central fells from Scafell to Bowfell. Coastal Cumbria and the areas east and northeast of the fells receive considerably less.

Precipitation falls on about 220 days per year, although daily amounts are not even and vary with location. About one quarter of the annual total falls in the four months March through June, and in excess of one half the annual total falls in the three months November through January. Writers are sometimes accused of giving the Lake District an exaggerated reputation for rain, but the data speak for themselves.

The *Cumbria Climate Change Strategy 2008–2012* claims that summer rainfall will reduce by as much as 15% by the 2020s and winter rainfall will increase by about 15% by 2050, and perhaps 30% by 2080. These figures are conditional on the continued discharge of high amounts of greenhouse gases into the atmosphere. If these predictions come to fruition then the words of Coleridge may be of even greater significance for Lakeland.

7.2 The Styhead Tarn rain gauge.

Rivers

The study of river processes and associated landforms is known as **fluvial geomorphology** (from *fluvius* (Latin) meaning 'river'). Most watercourses receive precipitation indirectly as a result of seepage from the soil or via springs. During periods of heavy rain and rapid snow melt water can flow across the surface (**overland flow**) to the river channels. Very little precipitation falls directly into the channels. Rivers transport water across the land surface to the oceans or inland seas. In so doing they erode materials from their banks and beds, carry it some distance, and eventually deposit it. They have been and continue to be a major agent responsible for shaping much of the landscape.

The Earth's rivers exhibit tremendous diversity in all their attributes. Geology, climate, topography, vegetation cover and land-use all contribute to this diversity. Many of the larger rivers flow across different climatic zones and may traverse several geological and topographical boundaries on their journey to the sea. As a result there is a great variety of landforms along the course of an individual river as well as between different rivers.

The term **drainage basin** (sometimes **catchment** or **watershed**) is given to the area of land drained by a river. Within each basin is a network of channels. Usually there are many tributary channels that join to create larger channels. The boundary of the basin is known as the **drainage divide** or **catchment boundary**. When seen on maps or from the air, it becomes clear that basins differ greatly in size and shape. Once again it is largely geology, climate and topography that determine basin characteristics.

At a global scale the rivers of the Lake District are rather insignificant features, but at a regional scale they are extremely important. They have not only created some very impressive landforms but can, and frequently do, interfere with human activities.

Undoubtedly the best initial means of examining the rivers of the Lake District is to study the 1:25,000 scale OS maps. The so-called 'blue-line network' provides an immediate overview of the drainage system in any particular valley. The style of the blue line is representative of the river width. Rivers exceeding 8 m in width are shown by two blue lines with a lighter blue colour between them; a single blue line indicates a river that is less than 8 m wide. A word of caution is needed here – do not confuse rivers with the north-south and east-west grid lines, which are also shown in blue – it has been done before to much embarrassment and amusement!

I do not know how many watercourses there are in the Lake District, I very much doubt if anybody does, not even those responsible for water supply. The total length of all watercourses is also somewhat of a mystery. Nevertheless, the maps indicate that great variation exists in both number and length of channels for individual valleys. For example, dense channel networks are present near Stake Pass in Langstrath, in Greenup, and at the heads of Mickleden, Ramps Gill, Deepdale, Rydale, and Kentmere. Other areas have rather sparse networks and there are some 1 km grid squares that lack those wiggly blue lines. My scrutiny of the maps has revealed 15 such squares wholly within the National Park (excluding squares that take in sizeable chunks of lakes); 10 of them are in areas underlain by limestone and are close to the Park's boundary. To locate these I recommend a dark, damp winter evening when there is nothing of interest on television; you will need great patience to work your way very slowly, square by square, across each map sheet.

Many of the larger Lake District watercourses carry the name 'river' whereas smaller ones are usually called becks, burns, gills (or ghylls), grains, gutters, or sikes, but a very large number are unnamed on the maps. Beck is the most common generic term for a Lakeland watercourse (about 200 examples) followed by gill (about 120 occurrences). Gills often become becks – Angletarn Gill and Allencrags Gill join to form Langstrath Beck; Stake Gill and Rossett Gill become Mickleden Beck; Yeastyrigg Gill and Rest Gill become Lingcove Beck. Farther downvalley these becks join with or become rivers. Sometimes the derivation or use of a name may not be immediately obvious. Why, for example, to the east and west of Walna Scar in an area dominated by gills and becks are two watercourses called gutters? Another two gutters occur in the fells to the north of Haweswater. How did Grainsgill Beck, a tributary of the River Caldew, get its tautological name?

We have seen in Chapter 3 that the basic drainage pattern of Lakeland probably originated prior to the **Quaternary** period and was then modified by episodes of glaciation. This section focuses on fluvial landforms that have been created since the **Late Devensian** ice-sheet disappeared; so we are dealing with the last 15,000 years or so.

During this time the rivers have undergone great changes. During and immediately following **deglaciation** the modern system of drainage was initiated. Vast quantities of glacial debris had been left behind and for about 5,000 years the rivers were able to erode and redistribute this material. Therefore, as with some of the **mass movements** considered in Chapter 6, the landforms created by fluvial deposition are, in effect, of **paraglacial** origin.

The short-lived **Loch Lomond Glaciation** interrupted river development in the upper valleys but at lower levels erosion and deposition of sediment continued, aided by meltwater from the small glaciers. With the rise in temperature that terminated this glacial episode and enabled woodlands to colonise and flourish, came a marked reduction in the ability of rivers to erode and transport sediment. Although we do not know how much precipitation the fell country received between about 6,000 and 11,000 years ago we can safely assume that much was intercepted by the trees and, as a consequence, the rivers did not rise and flood quite as quickly as they are capable of doing in the present, virtually, treeless landscape.

Things started to change about 6,000 years ago when Neolithic farmers began to exploit the landscape. Slowly the woodland was opened up to create land for agriculture. With the trees disappearing, precipitation that had been previously intercepted was able to reach the soil directly and either pass through or run across the surface to the river channels. During heavy rain the soils would have been more susceptible to erosion and the rivers more active. So began the transition to the landscape we see today and a long relationship (some would say fight) commenced between people and rivers.

In their upper reaches most rivers retain many of their natural attributes, that is to say they have not been greatly modified by human activities (7.3). Where rivers enter enclosed agricultural land that situation changes. Since Medieval times the control of rivers has become increasingly important; valley floors could not have been brought into production for arable or pasture without it. In their natural state rivers shift their courses and deposit sand and gravel on adjacent land. To combat this, channels have been straightened and banks have been strengthened, weirs have been constructed to control the flows, and where steep hillside tributaries meet the valley floor they are guided across the pastures to the main channel rather than allowed to spread across the land. Such fixed river

7.3 The River Derwent above Seathwaite in Borrowdale is not constrained but is allowed to wander across its floodplain and deposit boulders and gravel at will.

7.4 The dry bed of the River Derwent at New Bridge, Rosthwaite, in the summer of 1976.

courses can be seen in many valleys – the Derwent below Seathwaite, parts of Kirkstone Beck and Goldrill Beck in Patterdale, Howegrain Beck in Martindale, Trout Beck above Limefitt Park, Newlands Beck, and Great Langdale Beck and its principal tributaries Mickleden Beck and Oxendale Beck – all are examples of how critical river control has been. More will be said about these 'engineered' rivers in Chapter 9.

A final general point is worth making about rivers – they can sometimes be dry because of drought (yes, even in Borrowdale). The steeper hillside gills and becks are the first to dry up; flow in the valley floor channels is more persistent but this can also disappear as 7.4 shows. These conditions give good opportunities to examine the composition and structure of river bed and banks without getting soaked, but cannot be booked in advance!

Landforms of fluvial erosion

Flowing water creates a number of distinctive erosional landforms at a range of scales. The features develop because water is capable of dislodging bedrock and moving sediment – from tiny particles of clay to large boulders. As river flow is rarely constant for long periods, so the rate of erosion is not constant. Some erosional features can be produced during the passage of a single flood; others are the culmination of many years of fluvial activity.

7.5 a, Tray Dub, a bedrock channel in the upper reaches of Langstrath; b, An alluvial reach of Langstrath Beck.

Channel Types and Patterns

Fluvial channels can be eroded in both bedrock and **alluvium** (the name given to material deposited by rivers), and a river usually has both types of channel in different parts of its course. An excellent example of a Lake District river with both bedrock and alluvial reaches is Langstrath Beck. At the Tray Dub footbridge the river flows in a bedrock gorge (Tray Dub, 7.5a); downstream of here for about 1.5 km is an alluvial reach (7.5b), followed by the bedrock gorge of Blackmoss Pot; next comes another lengthy alluvial reach and then from Johnny House to the confluence with Greenup Gill is another bedrock gorge. Shortly after the confluence, the river (now called Stonethwaite Beck) enters an alluvial reach that leads to Rosthwaite and beyond.

Channels incised into bedrock may have been initiated along faults or other structural weaknesses in the rock. As mentioned in Chapter 4, some of the gorges were probably cut by **subglacial** or **proglacial meltwater** flows and the present-day river is simply following the route taken by its glacial ancestors. It is difficult to determine how much erosion has taken place in any particular gorge since the glaciers disappeared. As a rule, bedrock channels in the Lake District tend to occupy long stretches of watercourses in their upper reaches and short lengths in their lower reaches and to be more or less straight or slightly sinuous in plan (7.5a).

Alluvial channels are diverse partly because the alluvium in which they develop can itself be rather diverse. Fine-grained alluvium (silt and clay) is normally cohesive whereas coarse-grained alluvium (sand, gravel and boulders) is non-cohesive. The character of the alluvium is one of several inter-related factors that control the rate of erosion; the others are river gradient, bank vegetation and available energy.

Naturally straight alluvial channels are rare; **sinuous** and/or **meandering channels** are much more common (7.6). Where they are not constrained by artificial banks, alluvial channels can and do undergo substantial changes because alluvium offers much less resistance to erosion than bedrock. As a result they tend to wander across the valley floor. As mentioned earlier, such channel changes can be gradual, perhaps taking several decades, or may be associated with a single flood event that lasts

7.6 The meandering channel of Gatesgarthdale Beck, on the Buttermere side of Honister Pass. The adjacent road takes a sinuous course too.

for just a few hours. It is often instructive to follow the alluvial reaches of Lake District rivers immediately after a flood to see the changes that have occurred. When viewed from high vantage points it is sometime possible to see traces of abandoned, infilled and overgrown channels from differences in vegetation or by areas of standing water.

Why do rivers meander rather than follow a straight course? It has to be said that the jury is still out on this one but the interactions between water flow and bed and bank materials are considered to be highly significant. Water flow in a channel is not as simple as might be imagined. A noticeably agitated water surface indicates turbulent flow; conversely a smooth water surface is usually taken to indicate laminar flow. What we cannot easily see is the spiralling (or helical) flow that is also

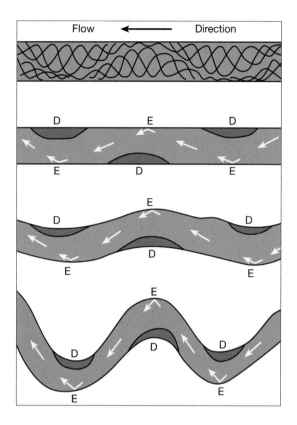

Flow ← Direction

D   E   D

E   D   E

E

D   D

D

E   E

E

D   D   D

E   E

7.7 Diagram showing
stages in meander
development from a
straight channel (top)
in which spiralling
flow interacts with the
banks to cause erosion
(E) and deposition (D).
Gradually a meandering
channel pattern develops
(bottom).

present in channels. Water moves from one
side of a channel to the other in that manner
and where it impinges on the bank it may
be capable of causing erosion, depending on
the nature of the alluvium. Material that is
eroded is usually deposited a short distance
downstream as a bank-side **bar.** Once established, these bars serve to deflect the flow
across the channel, so facilitating greater
erosion at those areas on the banks where
the flow is focussed. As a consequence the
river develops a more sinuous plan form that
may ultimately develop into a meandering
pattern (7.7).

Alluvial channels can also exhibit some
degree of braiding. A **braided channel** is
one in which the flow diverges and then
converges as it passes around bars and
islands (7.8). Several Lake District rivers
display this characteristic particularly at
times of low flow. During high flows, the
bars and islands may be submerged and the
flow occupies a single, wide channel. Braided watercourses are usually
associated with high river energy, steep gradients, abundant gravel and
boulders, and banks composed of similar coarse materials that are easily
eroded and enable the channel to shift sideways.

Bars are differentiated from islands by their lack of vegetation, which
usually indicates that they are susceptible to changes in size and shape
during floods (7.8). Islands are simply bars that have been colonised by
vegetation and are therefore more permanent features of the channel (7.9).
When a bar grows by sediment deposition to a height at which overtop-
ping by flood flows becomes infrequent, vegetation is usually quick to
establish and stabilise the debris.

In some places islands separate active river channels from other channels that are either dry or contain pools of standing water (7.10). These are
flood channels and, as the name implies, they are reliant on flooding for
generating water flow along them. The upstream end of a flood channel
stands a little higher than the normal flow height in the active channel. As
the river rises during heavy precipitation, water enters the flood channel
and flow commences.

7.8 A braided channel in which the flow divides to pass around a gravel bar.

7.9 A braided channel with a vegetated gravel bar (an island), a more stable feature of the river.

7.10 Flood channel on Stonethwaite Beck. The main channel of the river is behind the trees to the right.

7.11 a, Gullies cut into bedrock above Watendlath; b, Gullies cut into glacial sediment at Blea Water.

Gullies

There are numerous **gullies** on the Lake District fells; some are in rock, others in glacial sediments, some are deep, others shallow, some are straight, others twist and turn. Irrespective of their characteristics, they owe their origin to flowing water. In essence they are fluvial channels on steep slopes rather than valley floors.

Those etched deeply into rock (7.11a) are likely to follow geological structures and are probably very old, having been cut by powerful flows of **subglacial meltwater**, perhaps in more than one glacial episode. They provide sport for those who enjoy gill scrambling, and harbour trees and rare plants that can thrive because of the damp, shady conditions and the absence of sheep. Great Langdale is noted for its rock-cut gullies – Rossett Gill, Hell Gill, Crinkle Gill, Browney Gill, Dungeon Ghyll and Stickle Ghyll – are just a few.

Other gullies seam slopes of glacial sediment, as at Blea Water on High Street (7.11b). These, and similar gullies elsewhere, probably formed during and soon after **deglaciation** when there was abundant water from snowmelt and the slopes were bare. Today the gullies are almost completely covered by vegetation and although they still take water during bouts of prolonged rain the amount of erosion is very limited. Where did all the sediment from the gullies go? To the bottom of Blea Water of course.

Bank erosion

Bank erosion is one means by which a fluvial channel can migrate across the valley floor. Several processes can contribute, two of which were mentioned in earlier chapters – the growth of **needle ice** during cold conditions, and the (small-scale) **mass movement** of unstable bank material by falling or slumping into the channel.

Another distinct process of erosion is direct fluvial action on non-cohesive alluvium that makes up the banks. This material can be detached grain by grain, pebble by pebble. Where non-cohesive alluvium is overlain by cohesive alluvium that has a cover of vegetation, the river may cut a notch in the non-cohesive sediment causing large blocks of the cohesive sediment to overhang (7.12a). These blocks eventually break off (7.12b), drop into the water and may be carried a short distance downstream. A

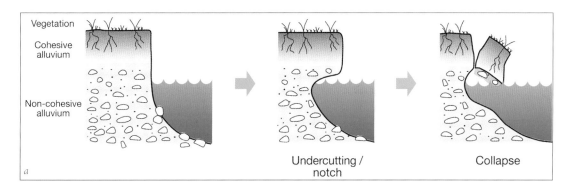

7.12 a, Illustration of bank erosion and collapse due to undercutting; b, Cracks like this alongside rivers indicate that undercutting has occurred and collapse of the bank is imminent. The survey pole divisions are 20 cm; c, Blocks of eroded bank material have been carried downstream by the flow.

good place to observe the results of this style of bank erosion is between Tray Dub and Blackmoss Pot, in Langstrath (7.12c). The presence of vegetation is important because the roots help to bind the material and provide additional resistance. Once they have fallen into the river the blocks undergo gradual disintegration.

Potholes and Fractured Boulders

Potholes are usually present wherever bedrock is exposed in the bed and banks of a river. Irregularities in the rock can act as traps for small stones that then get swirled around by the flow. This action causes **abrasion** to both the bedrock and the stones. Over time the irregularities get wider, deeper, smoother and more circular, and the stones become smaller, smoother and rounder. The enlarging pothole can then trap larger stones and the process continues (7.13a). Adjacent potholes may eventually merge and take on a variety of shapes.

7.13 a, Potholes containing stones in Pasture Beck. The survey pole divisions are 20 cm; b, River-side boulder showing two phases of impact fractures. The scale bar divisions are 5 cm.

Boulders in river channels tend to move downstream only at times of very high flow when they get trundled along the bed. Some of the very large boulders may never have moved since the glaciers or their meltwaters deposited them. Examination of boulders can often reveal the evidence for **impact** with other boulders in the form of fresh **fractures**. Boulders that do not move during floods gain fractures on their upstream face and sides because of impact from boulders moving downstream. The boulders that do move during floods usually show fractures on all their edges and faces as shown in 7.13b. Colour differences indicate at least two phases of fracturing are evident on this boulder – the left-hand corner shows a set of fractures that is more weathered and therefore older than those in the centre and on the right-hand side. Fracturing and abrasion are the means by which river boulders undergo reduction in size.

Terraces

A **river terrace** is a more or less flat area trending parallel to a river's course but at a higher elevation than the channel. Terraces result from fluvial incision; they can form in bedrock (**strath terraces**) or alluvium

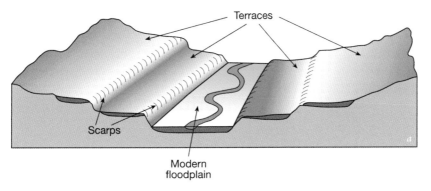

Terraces

Scarps

Modern
floodplain

7.14 a, Diagram showing the relationship between a river, its floodplain and terraces; b, River terrace in Mickleden with extensive and flat upper surface and steep scarp face (centre) rising above the floodplain. Rucksack for scale.

(**alluvial terraces**), and represent remnants of former valley floors. If several terraces are present they are usually separated from each other by a marked step or scarp (7.14a). In the Lake District, terraces can be seen in all of the major drainage basins but they are usually fragmentary and do not always occur on both sides of the river. This is because they have been removed by erosion as the river migrated across the valley.

A broad terrace exists on the northeast side of Mickleden (7.14b). It is a short distance from the track that leads to Rossett Gill and Stake Gill and a detour to see the scarp that separates it from the **floodplain** of Mickleden Beck takes only a few minutes. Several terraces exist in Mosedale (Threlkeld Common) and can be accessed by a walk along the Old Coach Road from St. John's in the Vale or Matterdale and then going north beside Mosedale Beck. But a walk along any of the principal valleys will reveal terrace fragments.

Terraces are indicators of rivers having adjusted to changes in circumstances. During **deglaciation,** meltwater rivers carried and deposited vast quantities of debris, choking the valleys with great thicknesses of material – the **sandar** of Chapter 4. Once the ice had gone and meltwater flows had ceased, the post-glacial rivers began cutting down into the sandar forming floodplains at lower levels and leaving remnants of the former valley floor perched as terraces.

In several respects fluvial terraces are similar to **kame terraces** (Chapter 4) and in some cases it may be difficult be distinguish them. However, hollows (**kettle holes**) can be present on the latter type of terrace but not on the former. Therefore they can sometimes be differentiated on the basis of surface morphology.

Peat Groughs and Haggs

Unlike the nearby Pennines and Forest of Bowland the Lake District fells are not smothered by expanses of wet, thick peat that are undergoing erosion. Nevertheless, peat is present locally and under normal circumstances these tracts do make for rather awkward conditions underfoot. I know of no one who actually likes squelching their way across the stuff; you never know if it is going to be ankle-deep or knee-deep. Wainwright noted several areas of eroding peat in the eastern, central and northern fells (7.15a) and referred to the ridge route between High Tove and High Seat as being '…not a pleasant walk…' and '…all swamps and peat hags.' (A. Wainwright 1958, *The Central Fells*).

Peat consists of the partially decomposed remains of dead plants that have accumulated under waterlogged conditions. It develops in areas that are cool and wet; hence it is usually abundant in the uplands, particularly on flat ground and slopes that are less than about 20°. Most peat has been accumulating for several thousands of years and is now a few metres in depth. Because it is draped across the landscape it is generally known as **blanket peat**.

Being a soft and wet material peat is very susceptible to disturbance and erosion. If the vegetation cover is broken and the underlying peat is exposed, erosion can proceed rapidly. Destruction of the vegetation can result from excessive trampling, burning or overgrazing. Most of the erosion is achieved by running water, although frost and wind may also play a part. On slopes erosion is manifest as parallel gullies or **groughs** (a term commonly used in the Pennines) incised into the peat mass. Where erosion has been severe some gullies extend down

7.15 a, The flanks of Wether Hill show signs of severe peat erosion; b, Close view of eroding peat haggs at Quagrigg Moss.

through the full thickness of peat into the underlying mineral sediment. On flatter ground the pattern of erosion is usually more intricate with gullies having many branches between which are mounds of peat known as **haggs** (7.15b).

The exposure of peat to the elements and its subsequent erosion have consequences beyond that of making your boots and lower legs wet and filthy as you attempt to pick your way across it. Water-borne peat fragments play a major part in helping to infill lakes and tarns, and also discolour drinking water. Excessive amounts of peat in streams and rivers can suffocate fish, while on the fells the farmers are losing grazing land. In addition, peat erosion is causing a reduction in biodiversity and a valuable scientific archive is slowly disappearing.

Landforms of fluvial deposition

Material carried by rivers is eventually deposited because of a decline in slope gradient and energy availability. As the flow reduces the largest particles are laid down first, smaller particles are laid down last and are usually carried a greater distance. Therefore **alluvium** often displays a gradation by size both horizontally (i.e. downvalley) and vertically (i.e. within the deposits). As a result of sediment deposition some very distinctive and large-scale landforms are constructed.

Floodplains

Areas of virtually flat ground are to be found alongside most river channels, except for those channels on very steep slopes. Such channel-side flats comprise the **floodplain** of the river. All rivers have floodplains but not necessarily along their entire lengths. In upland valleys floodplains tend to be fragmentary but with increasing distance downvalley they become more obvious landforms because they are more continuous and much wider. The relationship between a river, its floodplain and terraces is shown in 7.14.

As the name suggests floodplains are associated with periods of flooding. During floods sediment is both eroded by the river and deposited within and alongside the channel. When the water level in a channel rises and overtops the banks it is usually said that the river has 'burst its banks'. The water spreads across the floodplain and may remain there for several days until it finally drains away. Sediment carried by floodwater is deposited across the floodplain – larger particles are set down close to the channel, finer particles are transported farther away. Layers of sediment are quickly incorporated into the floodplain by the growth of vegetation and after a few months may no longer be visible. Over many years, repeated flooding causes a build-up or thickening of the floodplain so that eventually only the largest floods can overtop the river banks.

Floodplains change through time as the river channel migrates across the valley floor. Bank erosion at one point is usually compensated for by

7.16 a, Broad floodplain and gravel point bar in upper Eskdale; b, A relict point bar, with many boulders still evident, occupies part of the floodplain alongside Mosedale Beck, Threlkeld Common.

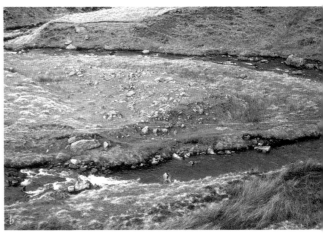

LAKE DISTRICT MOUNTAIN LANDFORMS

deposition at another as indicated in 7.7. These within-channel deposits are known as **bars** and may be attached to the bank or can occupy positions in mid-channel (7.8). Generally bars are dominated by gravel and therefore consist of much coarser materials than those laid down by overbank flooding. Probably the most common and easiest type of bar to recognise is the **point bar** that forms on the inside of meander bends as a result of localised bank erosion and the helical flow pattern (Figs 7.7, 7.12c and 7.16a).

It may seem that floodplains are rather uninteresting landforms – apparently just flat areas bordering a river. However, close inspection will more often than not reveal a variety of surface features that collectively demonstrate how the floodplain developed (7.16b).

As with **terraces**, floodplains are related to **sandar** having been fashioned from them as post-glacial river activity began to incise and redistribute their constituent materials.

Deltas

Where rivers enter lakes and tarns their velocity is reduced and their sediment load is deposited. The coarser sediment is deposited near to the shoreline in the shallower water, the finer sediment is carried farther and deposited in deeper water. Eventually the build-up of sediment results in the emergence of a tract of land projecting from the shore into the water body. The word **delta** was originally applied to the **alluvial** landmass at the mouth of the River Nile because of its resemblance to the Greek letter Δ (delta). However, deltas are not all the same shape.

There are numerous deltas in the Lake District. Most of the major lakes have several deltas; usually there is one at the head of the lake with others at various places along the shoreline where streams and rivers enter (7.17). Some deltas may seem to be rather large compared to the size of the rivers that created them. This may indicate that they have accumulated over a very long period, since the last glaciers disappeared, and that the river has had a plentiful supply of sediment to transport. Small deltas may reflect a paucity of sediment in the **drainage basin**, or a small basin area, or both. The absence of a delta around an inflow point may be because of deep water; the delta is there but is submerged. In these cases delta absence is apparent rather than real.

Many of the larger rivers and their deltas have been controlled and reclaimed in order to facilitate agriculture, building and tourism, as at Glenridding (7.17b). If left alone, rivers switch position as they construct

7.17 a, Deltas (centre and left of centre) at the south end of Ullswater; b, The Glenridding delta seen from high on the slopes of Place Fell; c, The Derwent delta at the head of Derwent Water.

their deltas. When channels get blocked by sediment during floods this may force the flow into adopting a different course. Abandoned channels can be seen crossing some deltas.

Delta morphology is also influenced by wave action. Waves, generated by winds, cause redistribution of some of the delta sediment and, as a result, beaches of well-sorted gravel particles front many deltas. The head of Wast Water faces directly into the prevailing southwesterly wind and this has resulted in the creation of a very impressive delta beach that extends in an arc around the head of the lake. Where deltas are no longer actively extending, perhaps due to a shortage of sediment, wave action is eroding the front of the delta and moving the material out into deeper water.

In some Lake District valleys there are bodies of delta sediment perched well above the water level of the nearby lake. These are **palaeodeltas** and were created during **deglaciation** when temporary lakes existed because of valley impoundment by ice. They are regarded as former deltas because they are attached to the hillside and they have flat or gently-sloping tops and steeper flanking slopes. The best examples are adjacent to the foot of Ennerdale Water, on the lower part of the southwest-facing hillside, at Croasdale and Gill Beck (7.18). During deglaciation the Ennerdale glacier had retreated part way up-valley but the escape route for meltwater was blocked by ice from Scotland that still occupied the Irish Sea basin and extended for some distance inland along the coastal plain of Cumbria. The upper surfaces of the Croasdale and Gill Beck palaeodeltas stand at elevations of approximately 200 m. This is about 85 m above the present-day level of Ennerdale Water. As the ice retreated and the level of the lake fell deltas formed at lower elevations. Another palaeodelta, described by Thomas Hay in the 1930s, is at Tenterhow Farm in the Glenridding valley. The delta surface is at 180 m, some 35 m higher than neighbouring Ullswater.

It is not known how extensive these temporary lakes were or for how long they persisted in the landscape, but it is likely that they were short-lived features. Nevertheless, the palaeodeltas are testimony to the rapid environmental changes that occurred during the decay of the Late Devensian ice-sheet.

LAKE DISTRICT MOUNTAIN LANDFORMS

7.18 Palaeodeltas near Ennerdale Water. The frontal slopes of the deltas are covered in gorse.

Debris Cones and Alluvial Fans

Debris cones and **alluvial fans** owe their origins to different processes but because they develop in similar topographic locations it is probably best to treat them together. Although they may form independently, in some situations cones grade into fans with increasing distance downslope and it can be difficult to determine the boundary between them.

The typical situation for cone and fan development is where a steep mountain stream meets a valley floor. At these points slope gradient is suddenly reduced and this promotes the deposition of sediment carried by the steeper stream. Alluvial fans also develop around points of confluence of major valley floor rivers.

Debris cones build up as a result of successive **debris flows**. These are, in effect, **mass movements** in which water plays a vital part, as in the open hillside **debris slides** of Chapter 6. Hillside talus and loose rock or glacial sediment in gullies are particularly prone to debris flow during heavy rain. Once the material is saturated it may start to move down the talus slope or gully as a water/sediment slurry. Many Lake District talus slopes show the scars of debris flows (7.19a). The smaller rock particles may be carried some distance beyond the foot of the talus and may be deposited on grassy slopes as parallel **levees** of gravel that delineate the flow track (7.19b). In gullies debris flows are constrained by the sidewalls, and only at the gully

7.19 a, Debris flows on talus below Clough Head; b, Parallel levees of gravel outline a debris flow track below Clough Head. The survey pole divisions are 20 cm.

exit where the gradient usually slackens does the slurry spread laterally and come to rest. Over long periods repeated flows have built up some very impressive debris cones, as at the foot of Little Narrowcove in upper Eskdale (7.20a) and the foot of Raise Beck on Dunmail Raise (7.20b).

An interesting set of smaller debris cones can be seen in the upper part of Rydale. On the west side of the valley, the upslope side of the wall surrounding Dalehead Close is obscured in several places by accumulations of sediment derived from hillside gullies (7.21). The age of the wall is not known with certainty but I'm reliably informed that it is an early wall – probably constructed in the seventeenth century. Irrespective of the wall's age the debris cones must be younger features. They are testimony to the rapidity of landscape change over the last 300–400 years.

Alluvial fans are products of fluvial sediment transport and deposition. Their surfaces are less steep than cones and in plan view they are triangular or fan-shaped accumulations. Many alluvial fans spread out onto low gradient slopes at the foot of debris cones and these are usually easy to identify. Fans that develop where valley floor streams meet are sometimes more difficult to recognise because they merge with the adjoining floodplain. A high vantage point on the valley side can usually provide the ideal view of these fans (7.22a).

Many cones and fans are almost completely covered by vegetation, an indication that at present they are not being regularly added to in any

7.20 a, Debris cone at the foot of Little Narrowcove in upper Eskdale; b, The Raise Beck debris cone on the east side of the A591 at Dunmail Raise.

significant way and that they are essentially relict landforms. However, bouts of heavy rain may result in large volumes of sediment being transported downslope coating the cone or fan in a layer of boulders or gravel, as 7.22b demonstrates.

Where streams have cut channels through cones and fans it is sometimes possible to find thin layers of peat sandwiched between thicker layers of sand and gravel (7.23). These peat beds represent times when the cones and fans were not receiving much sediment from the streams,

7.21 a, The upper part of Rydale. The upslope side of the wall at the lower left of the picture has a number debris cones built up against it; b, Part of the wall in Rydale obscured by a grassed-over debris cone.

7.22 a, Alluvial fan at the confluence of Grains Gill and Styhead Gill in Borrowdale; b, A tributary of St. John's Beck deposited this fan-shaped spread of boulders and gravel following a period of heavy rain.

7.23 A layer of peat buried by alluvial fan sediments near the head of Pasture Beck. The trekking pole is 1.1 m in length.

perhaps because heavy or prolonged rain storms were less common or because human activities such as woodland clearance or agricultural practices were not as intensive as they had earlier been. During these occasions peat formed on the surfaces of the cones and fans. When conditions changed and sediment deposition resumed the layers of peat were buried and preserved.

Samples of buried peat from cones and fans in the Pasture Beck valley, at Blindtarn Moss above Grasmere, in Keskadale, and in the valley of Roughton Gill to the north of Knott have been **radiocarbon dated** in order to provide a timeframe for peat development. A period of peat development common to all these sites is from about 1,100 to 800 years ago, coinciding with a time of benign climate. It is also just prior to intensification of land-use by Norse-Irish settlers that is likely to have disturbed the upland soils and caused the burial of cone and fan peats. In addition to their more violent activities the Vikings also had a geomorphological impact!

Fan-Deltas

Many steep mountain streams flow directly into lakes or tarns and the features they construct around the points of entry are known as **fan-deltas**. This term is used because the features comprise an alluvial fan, in their upper part, and a delta, in the area adjacent to and beneath the waterline, although it is not always easy to see where fan passes into delta. Examples occur alongside many of the major lakes with Buttermere and Crummock Water displaying several cases, including the tract of land south and west of Buttermere village that separates the lakes. A single lake existed here until Mill Beck decided to alter the local geography. The Hartsop fan-delta extends west across the valley; the area between Horseman Bridge and Cow Bridge has considerably reduced the northern extent of Brothers Water and has forced the outflow to run along the base of the steep wooded hillside. Three smaller fan-deltas can be seen at Styhead Tarn, two at the south end (7.24a) and the other at the foot of Aaron Slack (7.24b). The shape of the tarn owes much to the way these fan-deltas have spread into the waters.

7.24 a, Fan-deltas at the south end of Styhead Tarn; b, Fan-delta at the foot of Aaron Slack.

7.25 a, Wast Water – in a dramatic mountain setting; b, Windermere – in a pastoral setting.

Lakes

In spite of that old trick question 'How many lakes are there in the Lake District?', answer: one, (Bassenthwaite Lake), the rest are waters or meres, there are some 16 or 17 lakes. The exact number depends on whether or not you include Brothers Water; some writers regard it as a tarn.

It is the sheer diversity of the lakes and their settings that give the district much of its character and charm. The contrast between Wast Water (7.25a) and Windermere (7.25b) could not be greater, the former occurs below dramatic slopes of crag and talus, the latter has much more subdued shores of pasture, woodland and, at Bowness and Waterhead, urban development.

Windermere, at 17 km, is the longest of the lakes; Wast Water is the deepest at 76 m and part of its bed is below sea level, as are the deeper parts of Windermere and Coniston Water. Elter Water is the shallowest lake at 6 m. Bassenthwaite Lake has the greatest **catchment** area (238 km^2) as it includes the Derwent Water and Thirlmere catchments. Windermere is a close second at 231 km^2.

Surveys of lake depths were undertaken in the late eighteenth century, but the first comprehensive attempt to establish depths was by Dr Hugh Robert Mill and his results were published in 1895. Members of the Freshwater Biological Association (FBA) made further soundings in 1937–38. Together the surveys of Mill and the FBA allowed for

LAKE DISTRICT MOUNTAIN LANDFORMS

the construction of bathymetric charts that display the nature of the submerged topography. The 1:50,000 scale OS maps show bathymetric contours at intervals of 10 m.

The lakes are characteristically long and relatively narrow (Derwent Water is the widest, a fraction under 2 km) and owe their existence to valley floor erosion by glaciers – the **overdeepening** mentioned in Chapter 4 – and/or natural dams comprising **moraine ridges**. Bathymetric contours indicate that most lakes consist of a single basin but Windermere has two (termed north and south) and Ullswater and Esthwaite Water have three each.

Several lakes are at their deepest where glacier flow was augmented by additional ice from tributary valleys. The deepest part of Wast Water is a little way to the southwest of where glaciers from Over Beck and Nether Beck joined the main flow along the valley, and the combined ice-stream was constrained by the rock walls of Middle Fell and Illgill Head; the deepest part of Buttermere is near its head where ice from Honister Pass and Warnscale Bottom coalesced. The Ullswater basins are also adjacent to zones of ice-stream confluence. Overdeepening by ice was probably also favoured by local geological factors such as hardness variations and the density of joints and faults.

Recent geophysical surveys have indicated that the south basin of Windermere is considerably deeper than the 42 m measured in the 1930s. Strip away the sediments that line the basin, and from water surface to bedrock is at least 110 m. The lake surface is 39 m above sea level; therefore at its deepest point the basin is at least 70 m below sea level. The measured depths for the other lakes are only the water depths and therefore they are minimum indications of basin depth. There is still much to discover about the lakes.

Substantial moraine ridges exist at the southern ends of Windermere and Coniston Water and serve to contain the lakes in spite of having been cut through by the rivers Leven and Crake respectively. A submerged moraine ridge extends across Ennerdale Water just offshore from Anglers' Crag. Depending on the water level the highest point of this ridge is sometimes visible as a tiny island – Little Isle. Other lakes have much larger islands. Some of those in Derwent Water are probably **drumlins**, similar to the ones on which Keswick is built. In Ullswater and Windermere the islands are of rock and take the form of **roches moutonnées**.

Ullswater exhibits the greatest degree of departure from the relative straightness that characterises the larger lakes. The three segments of Ullswater, each with its own deep basin, are aligned along prominent faults in the bedrock; the glaciers took advantage of these weaknesses and produced the twisting valley form that is now occupied by the lake (7.26).

All the lakes have been reduced in area by the growth of deltas and fan-deltas. The separation of Buttermere and Crummock Water was mentioned earlier. Bassenthwaite Lake and Derwent Water are also believed to have once been a single lake but the River Greta and Newlands Beck changed the situation by building deltas that combined to divide the original lake. Over time the lakes have become shallower through the deposition of sediment. Most lakes have at least a few metres of the stuff but in the south basin of Windermere sediment thickness is about 70 m.

Two lakes, Thirlmere (7.27) and Haweswater result from damming and are reservoirs for Manchester. They are considerably larger and deeper than the lakes that were originally present. The Thirlmere dam increased Leathes' Water from 4.3 km to 6 km in length and from 34 m to 47 m in depth; the Haweswater dam increased High Water and Low Water from 3.8 km to 6.5 km in length and from 30 m to 60 m in depth.

Because specialised equipment is required to study the submerged features and sediment accumulations in lakes, many geomorphologists

7.26 Ullswater – a lake of three segments, each aligned along a fault in the bedrock.

7.27 Thirlmere – one of Manchester's thirst quenchers.

have to restrict their interest to shoreline features that can be easily seen. With a total shoreline length slightly in excess of 220 km the lakes provide ample opportunities for observing features that form at the interface of land and water.

Shoreline Features

Lake shorelines are probably the most neglected of areas in the Lake District with respect to geomorphology and yet they possess a variety of fascinating features that tell of changes that have occurred and, in some cases, are still occurring. Although certain lakes have shoreline footpaths, they tend to be a short distance from the water rather than immediately alongside, and much of interest is easily bypassed. During the 1920s and 1930s Thomas Hay described the lake shorelines at great length in a number of his articles, but since that time they have not attracted very much attention.

7.28 Tree roots exposed alongside Derwent Water as a result of shoreline erosion.

Lakes can have bedrock, talus, glacial sediments or marsh around their margins. Where glacial sediments are present, waves generated by strong winds are capable of winnowing the fine particles of silt and clay and carrying them out into deeper water. The coarser materials (sand, gravel and boulders) are left behind and form stony beaches. Excellent examples of this type of shoreline erosion can be seen at the western

7.29 One of Derwent Water's gravel beaches.

LAKE DISTRICT MOUNTAIN LANDFORMS

end of Buttermere and on the east side of Derwent Water near to the Watendlath road jetty. The erosion has been so severe that up to 50 cm thickness of soil has been removed from around a number of trees leaving their denuded, tentacle-like root systems exposed (7.28).

One effect of waves on stony beaches is to sort the particles by size. If wave energy is sufficiently high, small to medium sized stones can be thrown up the beach but the waves are only capable of carrying the smaller stones and sand particles down the beach in the backwash. Over time a distinction may become evident between the upper part of the beach with its larger stones and the lower part of the beach where the smaller material is concentrated (7.29). The effect is rapidly destroyed on those beaches frequented by lots of people.

On the west shore of Crummock Water there is a gravel beach that is unique in the Lake District in that it connects an island, Low Ling Crag, to the shore (7.30). The island is actually a roche moutonnée and the beach is about 50 m in length and is made up of flat pieces of Skiddaw rock most of which are 1–2 cm in length. This type of beach is known as a **tombolo** and is named after classic examples on the west coast of Italy. Tombolos usually form on the lee side of islands where there is some protection from strong wave action allowing beach sediments to build up. Offshore islands cause waves to refract (bend) – as the water gets shallower close to an island the waves slow down and their crests change direction and move parallel to the bathymetric contours.

7.30 Crummock Water's tombolo connects Low Ling Crag to the shore.

7.31 a, These large boulders in Ullswater are probably the remnants of a thick mass of glacial sediment eroded by waves; b, Aligned boulders near Glencoyne Bridge, Ullswater.

Large boulders, whether as individuals, small groups or great swathes, are present along several stretches of shoreline. Where steep craggy slopes rise above a lake, such boulders are likely to be the result of rockfalls, as is the case with the Wast Water screes or on parts of the Ullswater shore path below Place Fell. Where steep craggy slopes are absent a different explanation is required. In these situations the boulders are probably the remnants of a mass of glacial sediment that has been eroded by waves, the boulders being too large for the waves to move (7.31a). Examination of the boulders may reveal them to be a heterogeneous collection of rock types, so supporting a glacial origin.

Thomas Hay described examples of boulders that were arranged in lines just above the average water level of several lakes. He recognised that the boulders had probably been aligned artificially to protect the shore and the adjacent land from erosion. However, at Glencoyne (7.31b) and Gowbarrow on Ullswater he did not think this explanation applied for two reasons. First, the adjacent farmland had not been cleared of surface boulders, implying that it was not particularly valuable and in need of protection from erosion and second, the boulders were unlikely to have been moved during road construction because they are too far away from the road and would not have been manhandled that distance.

The explanation he offered was based on observations reported by geomorphologists from North America and northern Europe where lakes regularly freeze each winter. As great sheets of lake ice develop and expand they are capable of pushing large boulders towards the upper part of the beaches. The boulders are left there when the ice eventually melts. If this was how some of the Lake District boulder lines originated it was probably during a period with more severe winters than experienced today when the lakes were routinely frozen over.

Floating Islands

In some summers a **floating island** appears in the southeast corner of Derwent Water close to where Watendlath Beck enters the lake. It was mentioned as a curiosity in some of the early guidebooks, including Wordsworth's *Guide to the Lakes*, although he thought 'buoyant island' a more appropriate term.

The island makes its appearance during hot dry summers and consists of a slab of the material that normally occurs on the lake bed. It is believed that high temperatures result in greater amounts of plant decomposition on the bed of the lake and this liberates more gas, especially methane, which, in turn, causes the decaying material to rise to the surface as a buoyant mass (7.32).

In the nineteenth century the Keswick geologist and guide, Jonathan Otley, studied the island over a period of 20 years and described it at some length. The meteorologist George J. Symons published the results of his detailed observations in 1888 – *The Floating Island in Derwentwater*. He reckoned that the island had appeared on about 40 occasions between

7.32 a, Girl Guide and Union Flag on the floating island in the 1930s (photo supplied by Brian Wilkinson); b, A more recent image of a brave man (Chet Van Duzer) on the floating island (photo courtesy of Sandra Sáenz-López Pérez).

1773 and 1888, an average of about once every three years, and that its size varied from approximately 30 m² to 7500 m². It was also noted that the island could appear as early as June and it would normally have disappeared by October. I have not been able to find detailed records of appearances since 1888.

Most reports mention that the surface of the island is rather soggy, as might be expected, and therefore not recommended for standing on for too long, unless you like to have that sinking feeling. However, on one occasion in the nineteenth century the Keswick Town Band is reputed to have performed a concert on the island and on another, in the 1930s, the Keswick Girl Guides planted the Union Flag and claimed sovereignty for England! There are reported appearances of the island in August 2003 and July 2005.

Palaeolakes

It has been said on many occasions that the flat floors of many Lake District valleys are the beds of former lakes or **palaeolakes**. Given the number of times that the fields get inundated by floodwaters it is easy to see why this conclusion has been reached. Parts of Great Langdale (7.33), Borrowdale and Patterdale, mid-Eskdale and much of Longsleddale have been often been singled out as old lake beds because, prior to engineering works on their rivers, they were particularly prone to flooding. In some of these valleys it has been supposed that up to four former lakes existed, each impounded by a moraine ridge. However, the valley floor sediments are more typical of those deposited by rivers (**meltwater** rivers and post-glacial rivers) rather than having accumulated on lake beds. So the evidence for former lakes is not altogether convincing.

Much more compelling evidence for a palaeolake is in the form of the **palaeodeltas** on the hillside above Ennerdale Water (7.18). As the Ennerdale glacier retreated up-valley the escape route for meltwater was blocked by a great thickness of Scottish ice that still lay across the coastal lowlands. The meltwater simply formed a lake in the space between the two ice masses. The full extent of 'Glacial Lake Ennerdale', as this palaeolake is called, is not known for certain but the highest palaeodeltas indicate that its shoreline was along the 200 m contour, making it 85 m deeper than the present lake.

7.33 Great Langdale – often regarded as having held a lake.

Tarns

The delectable sheets of water scattered throughout the high fells are described in W. Heaton Cooper's *The Tarns of Lakeland* as 'the eyes of the mountain'. Few walkers can resist stopping, if only for a moment or two, beside a tarn. Some stop for longer, perhaps to eat their lunch, to have a swim, or to pitch their tent for an overnight stop on a multi-day mountain trek. Several of these will have made the tarn(s) the object of their day. Tarn-bagging may not yet have the same status as peak-bagging but *Exploring Lakeland Tarns* (Don Blair, 1993, Ellenbank Press) and *The Tarns of Lakeland* (John and Anne Nuttall, 1995/96, Cicerone Press, 2 volumes) have undoubtedly helped to popularise the activity. Wainwright also eulogised about some tarns and, as he had wished, his ashes were scattered beside Innominate Tarn on Haystacks.

The word **tarn** comes from *tjorn* (an Old Norse word for a small lake (another legacy of the Vikings!)). The word occurs in over 100 names although some of these refer not to sheets of water but to nearby features such as becks and crags. The exact number of tarns is difficult to ascertain – some do not have the word tarn in their name, for example Goat's Water and Blea Water, but they are undoubtedly tarns. Many others are unnamed. Blair lists 220 tarns, the Nuttall's claim that there are 335, and during the 1950s and 1960s two Grasmere residents, Timothy Tyson and Colin Dodgson, both now deceased, found and bathed in 730 Lakeland tarns.

Irrespective of the number there is enormous variation in the size, shape, depth and locations of tarns (7.34), and apart from their geomorphological interest and aesthetic value many tarns perform a valuable function as a source of water for either domestic or industrial purposes. Blair estimates that 40% of the tarns listed in his book have been modified. Artificial dams at the outflow of many tarns indicate that the level has been raised slightly and water is being abstracted.

Devoke Water is the largest tarn, covering about one third of a square kilometre; the smallest of the named tarns is Lang Tarn, to the north of Blawith Knott. Blea Water is the deepest, with a water depth exceeding 60 m; several tarns, including Foxes Tarn, Broadcrag Tarn and Boo Tarn, vie for the accolade of the shallowest – you would be unlikely to get wet much above the knees. Some tarns are found on summit plateaus (e.g. Red Screes and Kirk Fell), some are in cirques (e.g. Scales Tarn and Bleaberry Tarn), others are on ledges (e.g. Hard Tarn in Ruthwaite Cove and Lambfoot Dub above the Corridor Route), some occupy cols (e.g.

7.34 a, Angle Tarn, a cirque tarn below Bowfell; b, Angle Tarn, a ridge tarn above Patterdale, c, Loadpot Hill Tarn, a summit tarn; d, Hard Tarn, a ledge tarn in Ruthwaite Cove; e, Seathwaite Tarn, an enlarged tarn supplying water to Barrow-in-Furness; f, Blindtarn Moss, an infilled tarn above Grasmere.

Three Tarns and Burnmoor Tarn), some are on broad ice-scoured ridges (e.g. Patterdale's Angle Tarn and Eskdale's Stony Tarn), some are within areas of glacial sediment (e.g. Scandale Tarn, and Barfield Tarn to the south of Bootle) and others are within peat bogs (e.g. Launchy Tarn and

Redcrag Tarn). Broadcrag Tarn at 830 m on Scafell Pike is the highest tarn. Geology has exerted a strong control on tarn locations. About 50% of all tarns occur on rocks of the Borrowdale Volcanic Group, 40% are on the Windermere Supergroup, and 10% are on the Skiddaw Group.

Interest in the origin of tarns can be traced back to the latter quarter of the nineteenth century when Clifton Ward and Professor John Marr considered whether they were true rock basins scoured out by glaciers or simply expanses of water dammed by moraines. With very few exceptions tarn depths were not known but around the beginning of the twentieth century soundings made in tarns on Snowdon in North Wales clearly demonstrated the existence of rock basins. A logical assumption was that the Lake District tarns were also in rock basins. However, it was not until almost 50 years later that the systematic surveying of Lake District tarns commenced.

Between 1947 and 1960 most of the larger tarns in central Lakeland were surveyed by members of the Brathay Exploration Group. A further 15 smaller tarns were surveyed between 1980 and 1983. Haworth *et al.* (2003) tell the story behind this work in *Tarns of the central Lake District*, (Brathay Exploration Group Trust). Survey results demonstrated beyond any doubt that many tarns occupied rock basins and that depths were greater than had previously been imagined. A depth of 63 m for Blea Water was totally unexpected, only Wast Water and Windermere are deeper. The next deepest tarns are Levers Water (37 m), Grisedale Tarn (31 m) and Red Tarn on Helvellyn (26m).

The bathymetric charts show that whilst most tarns consist of a single basin, Patterdale's Angle Tarn has four, Hayeswater has three and Burnmoor Tarn has two. Cirque tarns, of which there are 19, are generally deeper than tarns that are not in cirques, and they tend to be deepest towards the cirque headwall rather than in the centre of the basin. These characteristics are due to the way in which cirque glaciers move. Because of the thickness of ice that develops, cirque glaciers undergo rotational flow and this facilitates erosion of a deep asymmetric rock basin. As the ice disappears the basin collects and retains water.

As with the lakes, the tarns have been reduced in depth and/or area since they formed. Examples of infilling by fan-deltas were mentioned earlier in this chapter at Styhead Tarn (7.24). Another huge fan-delta forms a very prominent feature on the east side of Hayeswater; Gray Crag provides an excellent aerial perspective of this. At a number of sites tarns have been completely infilled or drained and replaced by peat bog as at Blindtarn Moss, Dodd Bottom and Wolfcrag Moss. A walk across some of the ice-scoured terrain such as Grange Fell and Great Crag will take you across several small bogs that are sites of former tarns. At least one tarn (Keppel Cove Tarn above Glenridding) has disappeared as a result of its moraine dam being breached (more detail is given in Chapter 9).

Tailpiece

The *Cumbria Climate Change Strategy 2008–2012* was mentioned in the Introduction to this chapter. The document outlines the likely impacts on Cumbria based on predictions of temperature and precipitation changes. It is thought that flooding will become more common and place additional financial pressures on local authorities and the insurance sector. Whilst this cannot be questioned, and is probably of great concern to those who live on floodplains, there will also be corresponding implications for the rivers, lakes and tarns. River channels in particular are very sensitive components of fluvial systems and can undergo rapid change in response to heavy rainfall.

A greater incidence of high-magnitude flood events is likely to cause damage to structures that were designed to reduce the impact of less frequent and smaller-magnitude events (Chapter 9 takes up this theme). A new phase of river channel engineering work may be required to contain potentially damaging floodwaters (7.35). In the steeper headwater regions where channels have never been constrained the probability is that greater quantities of sediment will be shifted downstream. Alluvial fans, debris cones, and deltas may all begin to extend more noticeably as more sediment is moved. Lakeside flooding of roads, footpaths, beaches and farmland will also occur more often.

With all this extra water about it may seem a contradiction to mention the likely need for greater abstraction from lakes and tarns. But if summer rainfall is reduced the likelihood of seasonal drought increases. Domestic and industrial supplies may need augmenting and the lakes and tarns are an obvious target for obtaining what is needed.

The rivers, lakes and tarns of Lakeland have always been dynamic elements of the landscape; in the years ahead this may become much more apparent as they, and us, adapt to climate change.

7.35 Hayeswater Gill burst through one of its artificial levees following heavy rain and spread boulders and gravel across valuable agricultural land at New Year 2009. The stream should be flowing along the wide band of gravel extending from lower left to mid-right.

CHAPTER EIGHT

Limestone landforms

Introduction

U NLIKE PREVIOUS CHAPTERS THIS ONE is devoted to a specific type of rock and the landforms that are associated with it. Most of these features are unique to limestone and do not fit under previous chapter headings, hence the need for this one.

Carboniferous Limestone is not particularly common within the Lake District. The geological map in Chapter 2 (2.1) shows that it crops out in a narrow zone along the northern margin of the National Park from near Egremont in the west and then by Cockermouth and Caldbeck in the north, where it has broadened substantially, to Shap in the east. In the south the limestone outcrop is discontinuous as it extends southwest from Kendal towards the Leven Estuary.

Around its northern arc much of the limestone is buried beneath glacial sediment, but at Clints Crag near Blindcrake, and Heughscar Hill and Knipescar Common (8.1a) south of Penrith small but bold scarps are found facing in towards the central Lake District. Southwest of Kendal faulting has divided the limestone so it now forms the prominent west-facing scarps of Scout Scar and Whitbarrow (8.1b). Although these limestone hills are not particularly high and occur on the margins of the National Park, walking routes exist on all of them and are detailed by Wainwright in *The Outlying Fells of Lakeland*.

Limestone is a very hard rock and wherever it occurs has a tendency to create distinctive landscape with distinctive features. The study of these landscapes and landforms is known as **karst geomorphology**. The word **karst** is the German form of the Slovenian word *kras* and the Italian word *carso* – meaning bare and stony ground. As a result, karst regions are usually quite rugged, and characteristically they are dominated by slowly soluble rocks, chiefly limestones. Because limestone is soluble, surface water in the form of streams and tarns is normally absent – it mostly goes underground where, over thousands of years, it has created extensive cave systems with their associated stalagmites and stalactites. So karst regions are unique by virtue of having both surface landforms and subterranean landforms.

Glaciers have also played a part in shaping the limestone areas. As ice flowed away from the central Lake District the limestone terrain was subjected to plucking and abrasion but was sufficiently resistant to survive as upstanding ground in contrast to adjacent, less resistant areas. In recognition of the fact that ice has had an impact on these landscapes the term **glaciokarst** is frequently used.

Although the solution of limestone creates some very distinctive features the process of solution is an imperceptible one that does not cause sudden changes to the landscape, as happens with some mass movement (Chapter 6) and fluvial processes (Chapter 7). Nevertheless, limestone areas are undergoing change even if we cannot see it happening. Rates of surface solution have been calculated as less than 1 mm per year under current environmental conditions – so don't expect to notice any significant changes between your visits to Whitbarrow or Knipescar Common.

The focus of this chapter is the surface landforms of the limestone areas. Narrow caves probably do exist within the Lakeland limestone but they are not of the 'show cave' variety and cannot be accessed by ordinary mortals, consequently they are not considered here.

8.1 a, The limestone scarp of Knipescar Common – on the north-eastern edge of the National Park; b, Whitbarrow – a prominent limestone hill southwest of Kendal.

A variety of surface features characterise karst landscapes. They range from extensive areas of bare limestone occupying many square metres of ground to considerably smaller features that have been etched just a few centimetres into the rock.

I really should not say this but the limestone features of the Lake District are not a patch on those that can be seen in the Yorkshire Dales and by visiting one of the tourist caves the underground karst can also be appreciated.

Limestone Pavements

Probably the best-known glaciokarstic landform is the **limestone pavement**. This is an expanse of bare limestone, usually flat or gently inclined, that is dissected by prominent fissures (8.2). Pavements have intrigued geomorphologists for many years and numerous studies aimed at explaining their origin have been conducted. Glaciation has long been considered an important agent in the formation of pavements. Ice movement is thought to have scoured away the cover of soil and weathered rock that previously existed and, in so doing, exposed, plucked and abraded these extensive rock surfaces on which solution then acted and fashioned various features. But although this is a widely accepted mechanism it is known to be a little more complicated than that. It has been demonstrated that some pavements are relicts from the Carboniferous period and have been exhumed rather than created by glaciation and more recent solution.

During Carboniferous times limey muds with shells and corals accumulated in a shallow tropical sea. Later, sea level fell exposing the newly created limestone to the atmosphere and enabling vegetation to colonise the surface. The surface (i.e. pavement) was also subjected to solution and a variety of hollows, pits and narrow clefts were etched into the rock; knobbly mounds and irregular ridges separated the depressions (8.2a and 8.3). Sea level then rose, inundated the pavement, and another phase of limey mud accumulation was initiated. Geologists have determined that some 40–50 such cycles occurred, each lasting between 250,000 and 500,000 years.

These Carboniferous pavements are known as **palaeokarstic** surfaces and it may be possible to confirm that they are of this variety by looking along their inner edges where beds of overlying limestone form a prominent step or small cliff. If the pavement is a palaeokarstic one the various surface undulations will be continuous and will have been filled with the

8.2 a, Limestone pavement at Knipescar Common; b, Limestone pavement at Whitbarrow. Note the marked contrast in the surface morphology of the clints in these two photographs. The former pavement is a palaeokarstic one, the latter is not.

overlying limestone, and the zone of contact will be highly irregular (8.4). In these cases we can be certain that the pavement was created in the Carboniferous and has been exhumed. In contrast some other pavements are 'smoother' and any surface undulations are less pronounced and they do not continue below overlying limestone beds. These pavements are thought to represent glacial scouring and exposure of non-palaeokarstic bedding planes in the limestone.

Irrespective of their origin pavements are usually divided into roughly rectangular blocks by intersecting clefts. The blocks, known as **clints**, can be from 1 m² to as much as 100 m² in surface area. The clefts, called **grikes**, can be up to about 1 m wide at the surface and usually taper with depth; some may be 1–2 m deep (8.2).

Just to complicate things a little more – the palaeokarstic pavements have undoubtedly undergone some additional solution since they were exhumed by glacial action. Although the amount of post-glacial solution has probably been very restricted we can say, nevertheless, that these pavements are **polygenetic** – they owe their characteristics to processes and events that occurred in both the Carboniferous and the Quaternary periods.

Finally, that glaciers have passed across the these limestone areas is evident from the large erratic boulders of Borrowdale Volcanic, Windermere Supergroup and Shap Granite that are present at various sites (8.5).

LAKE DISTRICT MOUNTAIN LANDFORMS

8.3 A circular palaeokarstic pit at Knipescar Common. The scale bar divisions are 5 cm.

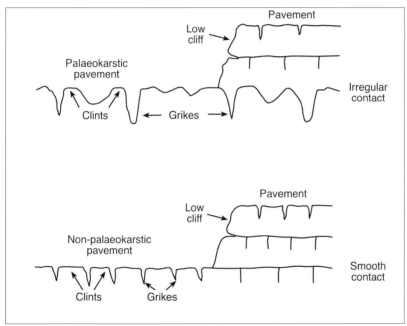

8.4 Diagram illustrating the differences between palaeokarstic pavements and non-palaeokarstic pavements.

8.5 Large erratic of Borrowdale Volcanic Group rock on the limestone of Whitbarrow. The scale bar divisions are 5 cm.

Karren

Features created by solution of limestone are known as **karren** – a German term for a host of diverse and elaborate forms that are differentiated according to their morphology. Some types of karren only develop on limestone that is covered by soil and vegetation; other types develop on bare rock. This allows a simple sub-division into covered forms and bare forms. Obviously the soil and vegetation has to be eroded in order for us to see the covered forms. As with limestone pavements, the complication is that once the rock is directly exposed to the atmosphere the previously covered karren undergoes modification.

Bare forms of karren have angular, often sharp edges and develop from direct contact with precipitation, whereas covered forms are smooth and rounded because the whole thickness of soil is damp and reacts with the limestone.

Although the presence or absence of soil and vegetation and the gradient of limestone surfaces can account for some of the morphological differences between karren features, the nature of the limestone itself is also very important. Suffice to say that limestone beds are not all of quite the same chemical composition or physical structure and this determines to a significant extent how effective solution can be at any particular site.

Probably the best-known types of karren are clints and grikes – or **flachkarren** and **kluftkarren,** to give them their alternative (German) names (8.2). Kluftkarren are generally thought to have been created along joints or fault-lines in the limestone. These would act as water seepage routes and over time they have been enlarged into the distinctive clefts we see today. Exactly how much of any individual grike is due to solution and how much is due to processes that created the initial joint or fault cannot be known, but solutional etching is usually evident along the sides of the grikes and tells us that this has contributed to their formation. There is still some debate whether clints and grikes are a type of covered karren or bare karren, but if grikes develop from water percolation along joints and fault-lines it is highly likely that they form in both situations. Under soil and vegetation, grikes will enlarge more rapidly than those on bare surfaces because of the acids derived from the plants and humus.

Rundkarren are a common form of covered karren. They are runnels etched into the top of the clints and are usually 15–50 cm in width and the same in depth. In cross section they are smooth and rounded and may have a straight, sinuous or meandering plan form (8.6a). Some rundkarren cut across the entire width of the clints, others terminate abruptly

8.6 Karren features from various parts of Whitbarrow: a, Rundkarren; b, Kamenitza; c, Rillenkarren; d, Trittkarren. The scale bar divisions are 5 cm and the lens cap diameter is 7 cm.

in a miniature valley head. On some pavements rundkarren continue from one side of a grike to the other, indicating that they developed before the grike opened. Essentially, rundkarren are drainage features even though they developed beneath soil and vegetation, and they can exist as single runnels or as more integrated networks. The orientation of the runnels is controlled by the dip of the rock surface. Wherever you see rundkarren you can be sure that the surface was previously covered with soil and that it has been eroded.

Solution pans or **kamenitzas** (8.6b) develop where limestone surfaces are horizontal. Rainwater collects in minor depressions and cannot drain away. Gradually the depression is deepened and widened by solution. Kamenitzas vary in size from a few centimetres in diameter and depth to 1 m in diameter and 10–20 cm in depth; they can range from circular to irregular in outline. Algae and fragments of dead vegetation collect in the pans where they decay and form a thin humus layer that provides acids and so assists with solution.

Rillenkarren are sets of narrow runnels or grooves, usually 1–5 cm in width and the same in depth, and up to about 50 cm in length, that are separated from one another by sharp ridges (8.6c). They develop on steeply inclined and vertical faces of limestone outcrops, are often regularly spaced and form quickly – within a few years – due to the direct contact of rain on exposed limestone surfaces.

Trittkarren are arcuate impressions on flat to moderately sloping outcrops of limestone. They resemble sets of heel prints in mud (8.6d). Typically the backwall will be no more than a few centimetres in height and the floor or tread is up to 20 cm in length. During periods of heavy rain the backwall can act as a mini-waterfall.

Dolines

Dolines (from the Slovenian word *dolina*) are enclosed depressions in the landscape and mark sites where water passes underground. They range from just a few metres to several hundred metres in diameter and are usually less than 10 m deep. Shape-wise they can resemble saucers, dishes, bowls, cones or cylinders. In northern England the alternative terms **sinkholes**, **shakeholes**, **swallow holes** and **potholes** are commonly used for specific types of depression; the term doline is all-embracing and avoids the need to explain the various processes of formation in detail!

Whereas all these doline sub-types can be seen in the Yorkshire Dales, those in the Lake District tend to be restricted to just two kinds and they are not quite as obvious as their Dales counterparts. Nevertheless, shakeholes are abundant on Moor Divock and Heughscar Hill to the west of Helton and Askham, the 1:25,000 scale OS map uses the term five times in an area a little over 1 km².

The shakeholes of Moor Divock and Heughscar Hill are **subsidence dolines**. In these cases the limestone is covered by glacial sediment through which precipitation has seeped and, by solution, has widened joints into which the sediment has gradually subsided and been washed down (8.7). Shakeholes are usually cone-shaped and may reveal some of the limestone on their side slopes and floor. Because the glacial sediment

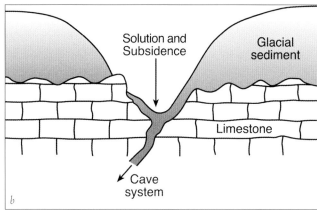

8.7 a, Subsidence doline on Heughscar Hill, west of Askham; b, Cross-section through a subsidence doline.

was deposited by the **Late Devensian** ice-sheet, the shakeholes have probably opened over the course of the last 15,000 years – since that ice mass disappeared.

The dolines on Whitbarrow are of a slightly different form and are known as **solution dolines**. Direct solution of bare limestone has occurred along joints, lowering the surface and creating broad depressions up to 10 m deep (8.8). The dolines may occupy sites where joints are quite closely spaced and have encouraged a greater rate of surface lowering. They are recognisable by their vegetation-covered floors and surrounding ring of low limestone scars or talus. A thin silty deposit known as **loess** is found on the floor of these dolines and is thought to have blown in from Morecambe Bay when sea level was considerably lower, between about 18,000 and 11,000 years ago. If that is correct then it implies that the dolines were already in existence. Given that Whitbarrow was covered by ice between about 25,000 and 18,000 years ago, the dolines must have formed before this most recent phase of glaciation, but just how old they are we do not yet know.

Gorges

Spectacular gorges are characteristic of limestone areas in Britain – for example, Gordale Scar in the Yorkshire Dales, Winnats Pass in the Peak District, and Cheddar Gorge in the Mendip Hills. Sadly, the Lake District cannot offer anything quite as stunning as these but it does have The Howk at Caldbeck.

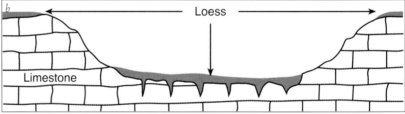

8.8 a, Solution doline
on Whitbarrow;
b, Cross-section through
a solution doline.

8.9 The Howk
– limestone gorge at
Caldbeck.

Just east of the attractive village, Welpo Beck cascades through a short and narrow chasm. In 1860 there was a natural limestone arch here but this has now collapsed. A 10 minute stroll from the village on a good path will take you to the ruins of a nineteenth–twentieth century bobbin mill beside the beck. Just beyond, the path ascends above the gorge to a footbridge that spans the beck and provides a dramatic bird's-eye view (8.9). It is probably best to go when the beck is in spate and is thundering through the narrow rock slot.

Another small but impressive limestone gorge is on the River Caldew, north of Hatcliffe Bridge. During droughts much of the water disappears down into the limestone reducing the flow considerably. Powerful rivers of glacial meltwater, heavily charged with abrasive rock particles, probably carved out both gorges.

In spite of being on the northern boundary of the National Park and away from the hills that bring people to the area, it is well worth devoting a little time to these gorges.

Tailpiece

Although the Lake District does not have much limestone the bits that it does have provide terrain that stands in marked contrast to the rest of the area. Bold white crags and pavements criss-crossed by fissures are the chief attraction. The ridge walking is generally easy (the ascent/descent of Whitbarrow will be the most taxing piece of ground encountered) and dry conditions underfoot are the norm. Limestone pavements can prove awkward when wet (they become very slippery) but that is no reason to shun them. The karren features, resulting from solutional etching, are just part of the fascination; another highlight is the abundance of plants that thrive in the grikes. You are likely to find as many botanists on limestone as geomorphologists.

In the past chunks of limestone pavement have been removed in order to 'decorate' domestic gardens. Fortunately this is now illegal. The best place to see and appreciate water-worn blocks of limestone is in their natural setting rather than as capstones on a boundary wall or components of a rockery. It is the same with fossils, with which the limestone abounds, once removed from their setting they lose all of their intrinsic value. The adage 'take nothing but photographs, leave nothing but footprints' probably was not coined with limestone in mind, but it certainly applies.

CHAPTER NINE

Man-made landforms

Introduction

People have been living in and around the Lake District for quite a long time although it is not known when they first arrived. Archaeological finds from several coastal sites between St. Bees and Walney Island indicate the presence of Mesolithic hunter-gatherers about 7000 years ago, but the effect that they had on the landscape is believed to have been restricted to some limited-scale clearance of the native woodland.

With the introduction of agriculture about 6000 years ago, Neolithic farmers required tools to clear the woodland and create grazings for their sheep and cattle, and to till the soil for cereal cultivation. So they began to fashion stone axe heads from some of the local rocks. It is with these Neolithic settlers that quarrying in the Lake District can be said to have begun and, as a consequence, people started to have an impact on the landforms.

Since Neolithic times there has been a significant increase in population and an elaboration of technology. As a result, the influence that people have had on the landscape has also increased and more than ever before they are able to both modify and create landforms. Such man-made features can be seen in virtually all valleys and on many of the fells.

This chapter deals with features associated with quarrying and mining, and the modifications that have been carried out to river channels, lakes and tarns, and some of the consequences of these activities. I am not concerned with buildings, roads and walls, in spite of these structures using materials from the quarries and contributing hugely to the character of the landscape. In order to include them the definition of 'landform' would have to undergo major contortion.

Quarrying and Mining

Evidence that Neolithic people exploited the Lake District's geological resources was found in 1947 high on the slopes of Pike o'Stickle overlooking Mickleden (9.1a). Amongst the stones of the south scree numerous roughly shaped axe heads were discovered, having been quarried from boulders of fine-grained volcanic tuff. These roughouts were probably discarded due to imperfections or were left behind when the site was abandoned. No finished axe heads (9.1b) have been found, suggesting that final smoothing and polishing were carried out elsewhere, probably at the coast. Langdale axes have turned up on archaeological sites throughout northern England, as well as in the Isle of Man, southern Scotland, Wales, and as far away as Dorset.

On the side of the gully overlooking the south scree of Pike o'Stickle is a small cave with vertical walls and a horizontal roof. Such a regular shape suggests that it is a man-made rather than natural feature. The cave has been linked with the Neolithic axe makers, but its age and origin remain to be established. Wainwright devotes a page to 'The Stone Axe Factory' in his chapter on Pike o'Stickle in Book 3, *The Central Fells*.

There are several other locations at which Neolithic people quarried stone for axes. Harrison Stickle, Martcrag Moor, Glaramara, Broad Crag and Scafell Pike have all yielded roughouts amongst their boulder deposits and testify to widespread stone working between 6000 and 4500 years ago.

9.1 a, Pike o'Stickle – site of Neolithic stone workings; b, Examples of a roughout (top) and a polished stone axe (bottom) from Langdale (photo courtesy of the Dock Museum, Barrow-in-Furness).

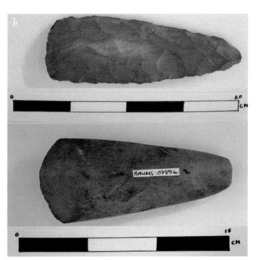

9.2 a, Loadpot Hole – a Roman quarry on the north side of Loadpot Hill; b, Part of the route of the Roman Road (High Street) on the flanks of Loadpot Hill.

Following the Neolithic period, quarrying seems not to have been important until Roman times. The Romans used locally derived slate to roof their forts at Ambleside and Hardknott, and on Loadpot Hill they opened a quarry, now known as Loadpot Hole (9.2a), to provide stone for their road that ran along the High Street range (9.2b). This former quarry is therefore the earliest example of medium-scale stone working in the Lake District. Wainwright thought Loadpot Hole was the site of a landslip – if it did result from a landslip then there should be a big pile of slipped rock in front of it – there is not, so it is unlikely to be so.

The Romans may also have been the first to mine certain of the various metal ores that occur in the district; some iron smelting was probably carried out at Hardknott Fort. However, following the decline of Roman authority in Britain in the fifth century AD another 700–1100 years were to pass before both quarrying and mining in the Lake District started in earnest.

Slate quarrying was revived in Norman times in order to provide roofing material for some of the great ecclesiastical buildings of the period and, by the seventeenth century, the quarrying and mining of rock had become a very important industry as a result of the growing trend of rebuilding in stone. Difficulties with transporting stone across rugged terrain resulted in numerous small quarries being opened in order to satisfy local demand. At the same time, larger-scale workings were established at Kentmere, Troutbeck, Coniston and Honister, with slate and facing stone being used in many parts of Britain and, later, overseas.

9.3 a, Slate spoil at Dubs Quarry on Fleetwith Pike; b, Partly-vegetated lead-rich spoil at Greenside.

In the sixteenth century, the Company of Mines Royal was established and German miners were brought in to exploit copper ores in the Newlands valley, around Coniston and in the Caldbeck fells. Lead was another important metal and its principal ore galena was mined at various places including Greenside above Glenridding. At one time Greenside was one of the richest lead mines in the north of England.

Ore mining declined at various times in the nineteenth and twentieth centuries. The last working metal mine, Force Crag in Coledale, closed in 1992. Stone extraction also declined dramatically during the twentieth century, and although it persists in a number of places it is but a fraction of what it was 100 years ago. However, the legacy of quarrying and mining remains for all to see in the spoil heaps, tunnels, shafts, quarry faces, trackways, leats and abandoned machinery. Many of the smaller quarry and mine spoil heaps are now overgrown and are being absorbed nature. The larger ones are still obvious in the landscape; some people see them as eyesores others view them as valued industrial heritage. It is not generally well known that English Heritage has scheduled the Coniston copper mines as an historical monument.

There is also the landform heritage created by quarrying and mining. Industrial landforms do not usually figure in geomorphological texts but geomorphologists are often consulted on the best ways of reclaiming and reshaping them and making them blend in with or mimic the adjacent terrain.

Spoil heaps are probably the most visually intrusive of the industrial landforms. Waste heaps of slates are often arranged like giant steps on the hillside. If you have been on Borrowdale's Castle Crag or to High Spy via Rigg Head, for example, you will be familiar with these features. Where slate working is ongoing or has recently ceased, the piles of tiered spoil are extremely prominent (9.3a). In order to make them fit more naturally into the landscape their slopes need regrading, and soil and vegetation should be encouraged. Some attempts to stabilize and reclaim metalliferous waste have been made at Greenside (9.3b). This has been quite a challenge because the toxic nature of the lead spoil means that vegetation is slow to establish. It is not a perfect solution, but other than put the stuff back where it came from or remove it completely (to where?) it is probably the best that can be expected. But it certainly does not blend in!

Large-scale quarrying and mining have also created some big holes in the ground. Many of these are deep below the surface and their combined volume can only be guessed at. Others are open to the surface like the 'cave' on Loughrigg Terrace above Rydal Water (9.4a). Wainwright thought that it was large enough to shelter the entire population of Ambleside. There is also the tremendous hole of Hodge Close Quarry in Little Langdale – 100 m in depth, half of which is below water.

Where some mine workings (levels) came close to the ground surface collapse or subsidence has resulted in large holes. Such holes can be seen in the Calbeck fells but perhaps the best examples are those at Greenside (9.4b). Although the 1:25,000 scale OS map indicates these as old quarries they do in fact result from an enormous collapse into the mine workings in 1862. Fortunately no one was killed, the collapse happened on a Sunday and the mine was shut.

9.4 a, Rydal 'Cave' – a former slate quarry on Loughrigg Fell; b, Holes created by subsidence into mine workings at Greenside.

Another consequence of mining at Greenside is the very obvious shoreline at Red Tarn below Helvellyn (9.5a). An earth dam was constructed at Red Tarn in 1860, as part of the water supply scheme for the mines, raising the water level by about 2 m. By 1936 the supply from Red Tarn was no longer essential so the dam was partly dismantled allowing the tarn to revert to its natural level. The shoreline is more evident on the south side of the tarn where the ground slope is steeper and it stands out because there are many large boulders that have not yet been obscured by the growth of vegetation (9.5b).

9.5 a, Red Tarn below Helvellyn has a very prominent shoreline running around its southern side; b, Closer view of the Red Tarn shoreline showing numerous large boulders. The modern shoreline is the narrow stony strip just above the water level.

9.6 a, A borrow pit for walling stone on Hartsop Dodd; b, A borrow pit for road stone beside the Wrynose Pass.

In some valleys quarry and mine wastes have been eroded by streams and deposited elsewhere. Writing in 1930 Thomas Hay provided some data about the growth rate of deltas whose streams carried such waste. The delta at Glenridding, which we saw in Chapter 7 (7.17b), extended itself by 76 m between 1859 and 1913, a growth rate of 1.4 m per year. Waste from Greenside Mine was responsible for this.

Scattered around the Lake District are numerous small excavations from which stone was removed for different purposes. These usually go unnoticed but once you have seen a few of the various types you will begin to recognise many more of them. The term 'borrow pit' is commonly used for these shallow depressions. They may have been opened to provide walling stone (9.6a) or road stone (9.6b).

9.7 a, The engineered channel of Oxendale Beck; b, Bank strengthening using rock 'armour', Stonethwaite Beck.

River Engineering

With the Lake District's frequent and abundant rainfall and predictions of more to come in the years ahead there has been and will continue to be a need to protect people and property from flooding. The control of water was a key element for settled farming, and there are monastic (thirteenth–fifteenth centuries) records of embankment construction designed to reduce the inundation of valley floor pastures for the area between Brothers Water and Ullswater. Now, virtually all of the Lake District's trunk streams and many smaller tributaries are constrained to some extent over various lengths. The purpose of this management is to get the water away as quickly as possible and in order to do that successfully river channels have to be efficient at moving water. Whilst this can be achieved it sometimes causes problems for people and property farther downstream, and it does not help that towns around the margins of the National Park are located on floodplains – as the residents of Cockermouth and Kendal know to their cost. Floods are natural events that are often exacerbated by human activities.

Techniques for controlling excess water usually involve the widening, straightening and strengthening of a channel, as was done some years ago for the flood-prone Oxendale Beck in Great Langdale (9.7a). The new channel lacks charm and many of the natural **fluvial** elements, but flooding in this part of the valley has been reduced. Bank strengthening using rock 'armour' has been undertaken along part of Stonethwaite Beck upstream of the hamlet (9.7b). The rapidity of bank undercutting and collapse meant that land was being lost to the river.

Rivers that flood frequently and carry a large sediment load tend to build natural embankments – known as levees – alongside their channels. It seems logical therefore that artificial levees should be part of water management schemes (9.8a). The raising of levees is, in effect, deepening the channel and helping to contain the floodwater. On occasions levees are overtopped or breached as mentioned at the end of Chapter 7 and shown in 7.35. Some levees are indicated by the 'earthwork' symbol on the 1:25,000 scale OS maps. Look, for example, at the River Esk upstream of Muncaster Bridge and Newlands Beck downstream of the A66.

Flood alleviation works may include areas designed to store water and release it slowly so as to reduce its impact on the channel and surrounding land. A small storage pond was created on Oxendale Beck just upstream of the artificial channel shown in 9.7a. This pond also collects coarse sediment and prevents it from travelling any farther and blocking or damaging the channel. A larger water storage area exists on the edge of Keswick. Where the Portinscale footpath leaves the road at Greta Bridge the fields are embanked and sluices enable excess water to be diverted and stored temporarily (9.8b). These areas are termed **washlands** and their purpose is to lessen flood severity.

9.8 a, A levee alongside St. John's Beck; b, Flood defences (water storage area, embankment and sluices) near Greta Bridge, Keswick.

9.9 a, A corner of Tarn Hows. The tarn is an amalgamation of three smaller tarns; b, The breached moraine dam at Keppel Cove. The former tarn bed is now rush-infested.

Lakes and Tarns

Lakes and tarns get a brief mention in this chapter because many have been modified and some are entirely artificial. This point should be remembered whenever there is argument over proposed developments in the National Park. The creation of Thirlmere and Haweswater was commented on in Chapter 7. Ennerdale Water and Crummock Water have also had their levels raised slightly by the construction of discreet dams.

Some tarns have also been created or enlarged. Scope Beck Tarn, Yew Tree Tarn and several of the Claife Heights tarns are examples of the former; Hayeswater, Stickle Tarn and Blea Water are examples of the latter. But probably the best known and most loved of the enlarged tarns is Tarn Hows (9.9a). This was created in 1865 when James Marshall of Monk Coniston Hall amalgamated three smaller tarns by means of a dam. The estate was bought by Mrs. Heelis (better known as Beatrix Potter) in 1929 and is now a National Trust property. I doubt if many of the visitors to Tarn Hows know that it is not entirely natural. I also doubt that many would want to see the dam dismantled and the area returned to its original condition, such is the affection in which it is held. The jigsaw, calendar and postcard industry would go into decline!

Other tarns are either no longer present or are substantially smaller, having been drained. The dam at Keppel Cove Tarn above Glenridding was breached during heavy rain in the early hours of 29th October 1927. A **moraine** ridge impounded the tarn, although this had been modified in order that Greenside Mine could draw off water. The V-shaped breach in the moraine is about 10 m deep and 30 m wide at the top and the former tarn bed is now rush-infested (9.9b). A replacement concrete dam was built a short distance downstream of the moraine dam but in 1931 this was also breached. Both of the resulting floods caused extensive damage in Glenridding.

Just over the ridge of Stang to the northeast of Keppel Cove is the now drained Sticks Tarn (aka Top Dam). The original shallow tarn was enlarged by damming, again in order to supply Greenside Mine with water. Several diagrams in Wainwright's 1955 *Eastern Fells* depict the tarn. When the mine closed in 1962 part of the dam was dismantled causing the tarn to empty.

Tailpiece

The impact that people have had on landforms is not as marked as the impact they have had on other facets of the Lake District. Only a few people would dispute the attractiveness of the present-day agricultural landscape divided, as it is, by dry-stone walls, cropped by Herdwicks, Rough Fells and Swaledales, and dotted with stone-built farmhouses and barns. And yet this scene is entirely man-made – the result of many years of hard graft by countless generations of landowners and tenant farmers. Therefore we are hardly in a position to question the creation, modification and/or destruction of landforms. This is especially so when, as we have seen, the landform changes have in most respects been done in order to complement and sustain the agricultural way of life.

CHAPTER TEN

Finale

I N CHAPTER I THE PHOTOGRAPH of the Langdale Pikes (1.1) was used to make the point that any view of the Lake District shows a variety of distinctive geomorphological features. Now, having worked your way through the different chapters you should be able to return to that photograph and recognise a range of diverse landforms and understand how and when most of them were created. However, rather than thumbing your way back to page 2 the photograph is reproduced here as 10.1.

Perhaps the most obvious feature is the valley itself. It has steep, rugged side slopes and a flat floor and has undoubtedly been carved by ice. It is one of many **glacial troughs** in the Lake District, but the alignment of the valley was probably determined by geological structures and **fluvial** activity prior to the phases of glaciation; the glaciers modified a pre-existing valley. On close inspection the valleyside crags show evidence for glacial **plucking** and **abrasion**, and some are good examples of **roches moutonnées**. The valley floor is a **sandur** composed of **proglacial** sediment that has been modified by more recent fluvial activity and enclosed for agricultural purposes.

Since the last glacier disappeared from Langdale some of the valleyside crags have released large quantities of rock that now form sheets of **talus**. Whether the talus accumulated as a consequence of **periglacial** or **paraglacial** processes is not always easy to determine. The Copt How boulders, seen in the foreground of 10.1, may also be a product of **rockfall** from valleyside crags; an alternative explanation is that they represent a cluster of **erratics** deposited by that last glacier. We do not yet know the origin of all the landforms in the Lake District and in those cases we have to acknowledge the fact.

Nevertheless these are just a selection of the geomorphological features that make up Great Langdale; from a different viewpoint additional features would be evident. 10.2 attempts to put many of these features

10.1 Great Langdale and the Langdale Pikes. This much-admired Lake District scene is composed of a mosaic of distinctive landforms.

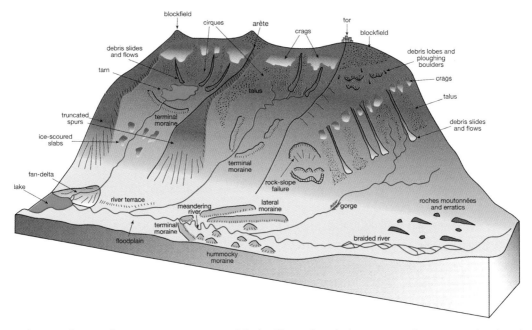

10.2 Schematic diagram that attempts to put some of the landforms described in previous chapters into their broader landscape context.

into their broader landscape context and 10.3 is selection of scenes for which you should be able to provide geomorphological explanations.

Hopefully you will now appreciate that the Lake District landscape (and any landscape for that matter) is a mosaic of landforms, each with its own history and relationship to adjacent features. With careful observation a fascinating landscape story can be teased out.

10.3 (opposite) What geomorphological features do you recognise in each of these photos? a, Hayeswater; b, Upper Eskdale; c, On Fleetwith Pike; d, Below Striding Edge; e, In Dungeon Ghyll; f, In Ruthwaite Cove; g, Warnscale Bottom; h, Styhead Gill.

Further Reading

FOR THOSE READERS wanting to know and understand more about the landforms of the Lake District the references listed below provide additional details. Some of the references are academic research publications and can be accessed through university libraries or geological societies; others may be obtained through public libraries.

Although some of the references can be considered 'old' (dating from before 1970) this does not necessarily mean that the information they contain on landform development is out-dated – in spite of the view held by some geomorphologists that publications pre-dating their own date of birth should be treated with a great deal of scepticism! In those cases where it is generally accepted that earlier theories can no longer be sustained, the references provide interesting insights concerning the development of ideas and paradigm shifts.

General

Beale, S. & Dodd, M. (eds). 2008. *Exploring Lakeland rocks and landscapes*. Cumberland Geological Society.

Boardman, J. 1992. Quaternary landscape evolution in the Lake District – a discussion. *Proceedings, Cumberland Geological Society* 5, 285–315.

Boardman, J. 1996. *Classic landforms of the Lake District*. The Geographical Association, Sheffield.

Clark, R. & Wilson, P. 1997. Characteristics and origins of Late Quaternary landforms and sediments at Carrock Fell End. In: Boardman, J. (ed.), *Geomorphology of the Lake District: a field guide*. British Geomorphological Research Group, Oxford, 37–49.

Clark, R. & Wilson, P. 2001. Origin of some slope-foot debris accumulations in the Skiddaw upland, northern Lake District. *Proceedings of the Yorkshire Geological Society* 53, 303–310.

Clark, R. & Wilson, P. 2002. Landform studies in Mosedale, northeastern Lake District: opportunities for field investigations. *Field Studies* 10, 177–206.

Dodd, M. (ed.). 1992. *Lakeland rocks and landscape: a field guide*. Ellenbank Press, Maryport.

Hay, T. 1937. Physiographical notes on the Ullswater area. *Geographical Journal* 90, 426–445.

Hay, T. 1942. Physiographical notes from Lakeland. *Geographical Journal* 100, 165–173.

Hay, T. 1943. Notes on glacial erosion and stone stripes. *Geographical Journal* 102, 13–20.

Hay, T. 1944. Rosthwaite moraines and other Lakeland notes. *Geographical Journal* 103, 119–124.

Huddart, D. & Glasser, N.F. 2002. *Quaternary of Northern England*. Geological Conservation Review Series, No. 25, Joint Nature Conservation Committee, Peterborough.

King, C.A.M. 1976. *Northern England*. Metheun, London.

Monkhouse, F.J. 1972. *The English Lake District*. The Geographical Association, Sheffield.

Pearsall, W.H. & Pennington, W. 1973. *The Lake District: a landscape history*. Collins, London.

Pennington, W. 1978. Quaternary geology. In: Moseley, F. (ed.), *Geology of the Lake District*. Yorkshire Geological Society, Occasional Publication No. 3, 207–225.

Smith, A. 2004. *Landscapes around Keswick*. The Landscapes of Cumbria No. 2, Rigg Side Publications, Keswick.

Vincent, P. 1985. Quaternary geomorphology of the southern Lake District and Morecambe Bay area. In: Johnson, R.H. (ed.), *The geomorphology of northwest England*. Manchester University Press, Manchester, 159–177.

Geological background

Cooper, A.H., Rushton, A.W.A., Molyneux, S.G., Hughes, R.A., Moore, R.M. & Webb, B.C. 1995. The stratigraphy, correlation, provenance and palaeo-geography of the Skiddaw Group (Ordovician) in the English Lake District. *Geological Magazine* 132, 185–211.

Johnson, E.W., Soper, N.J., Burgess, I.C., Ball, D.F., Beddoe-Stephens, B., Carruthers, R.M., Fortey, N.J., Hirons, S.R., Merritt, J.W., Millward, D., Molyneux, S.G., Roberts, B., Rushton, A.W.A., Walker, A.B. & Young, B. 2001. *Geology of the country around Ulverston*. Memoir of the British Geological Survey, Sheet 48 (England and Wales).

Millward, D., Johnson, E.W., Beddoe-Stephens, B., Young, B., Kneller, B.C., Lee, M.K., Fortney, N.J., Allen, P.M., Branney, M.J., Cooper, D.C., Hirons,

S., Kokelaar, B.P., Marks, R.J., McConnell, B.J., Merritt, J.W., Molyneux, S.G., Petterson, M.G., Roberts, B., Rundle, C.C., Rushton, A.W.A., Scott, R.W., Soper, N.J. & Stone, P. 2000. *Geology of the Ambleside district*. Memoir of the British Geological Survey, Sheet 38 (England and Wales).

Moseley, F. (ed.). 1978. *Geology of the Lake District*. Yorkshire Geological Society, Occasional Publication No. 3.

Pettersen, M.G. 1990. Recent developments concerning the Borrowdale Volcanic Group of the English Lake District. *Proceedings, Cumberland Geological Society* 5, 151–168.

Smith, A. (ed.) 2001. *The rock men: pioneers of Lakeland geology*. Cumberland Geological Society.

Woodhall, D.G. 2000. *Geology of the Keswick district*. Sheet description of the British Geological Survey, 1:50,000 series sheet 29 Keswick (England and Wales).

The pre-glacial landscape

Clark, R. 1988. Pattern and order in the Lake District landscape. *Proceedings, Cumberland Geological Society* 5, 17–34.

Clark, R. 1994. The Skiddaw Massif problem. *Proceedings, Cumberland Geological Society* 5, 437–448.

Clark, R. 2004. How old is the Lake District landscape? *Proceedings, Cumberland Geological Society* 7, 37–45.

Clark, R. 2004. The distinctiveness of the southern Lake District landscape. *Proceedings, Cumberland Geological Society* 7, 46–57.

Hay, T. 1944. Mountain form in Lakeland. *Geographical Journal* 103, 263–271.

Hollingworth, S.E. 1936. High level erosional platforms in Cumberland and Furness. *Proceedings of the Yorkshire Geological Society* 23, 159–177

Hollingworth, S.E. 1938. The recognition and correlation of high-level erosion surfaces in Britain: a statistical study. *Quarterly Journal of the Geological Society* 94, 55–84.

Linton, D.L. 1957. Radiating valleys in glaciated lands. Reprinted in: Embleton, C. (ed.), *Glaciers and glacial erosion*. Macmillan, 1972, 130–148.

McConnell, R.B. 1939. Residual erosion surfaces in mountain ranges. *Proceedings of the Yorkshire Geological Society* 24, 76–98.

McConnell, R.B. 1940. Relic surfaces in the Howgill Fells. *Proceedings of the Yorkshire Geological Society* 24, 152–164.

Mitchell, G.H. 1931. The geomorphology of the eastern part of the Lake District. *Proceedings of the Liverpool Geological Society* 15, 322–338.

Parry, J.T. 1960. The erosion surfaces of the south-western Lake District. *Transactions of the Institute of British Geographers* 28, 39–54.

Glaciation and related landforms

Ballantyne, C.K., Stone, J.O. & Fifield, L.K. 2009. Glaciation and deglaciation of the SW Lake District, England: implications of cosmogenic ^{36}Cl exposure dating. *Proceedings of the Geologists' Association* 120, 139–144.

Boardman, J. 1982. Glacial geomorphology of the Keswick area, northern Cumbria. *Proceedings, Cumberland Geological Society* 4, 115–134.

Boardman, J. 1991. Glacial deposits in the English Lake District. In: Ehlers, J., Gibbard, P.L. & Rose, J. (eds), *Glacial deposits of Great Britain and Ireland*. Balkema, Rotterdam, 175–183.

Clark, R. 1990. On the last glaciation of Cumbria. *Proceedings, Cumberland Geological Society* 5, 187–208.

Clark, R. 2006. On identifying frontal positions of Lake District valley glaciers. *Proceedings, Cumberland Geological Society* 7, 162–176.

Clark, R. & Wilson, P. 1994. Valley moraines in Borrowdale. In: Boardman, J. & Walden, J. (eds), *The Quaternary of Cumbria: field guide*. Quaternary Research Association, Oxford, 153–156.

Clough, R.M. 1977. Some aspects of corrie initiation and evolution in the English Lake District. *Proceedings, Cumberland Geological Society* 3, 209–232.

Evans, I.S. 1994. Cirques and moraines of the northern fells, Cumbria: Bowscale and Bannerdale. In: Boardman, J. & Walden, J. (eds), *The Quaternary of Cumbria: field guide*. Quaternary Research Association, Oxford, 129–142.

Evans, I.S. 1997. Cirques and moraines of the Helvellyn range, Cumbria: Grisedale and Ullswater. In: Boardman, J. (ed.), *Geomorphology of the Lake District: a field guide*. British Geomorphological Research Group, Oxford, 63–87.

Evans, I.S. & Cox, N.J. 1995. The form of glacial cirques in the English Lake District, Cumbria. *Zeitschrift für Geomorphologie* 39, 175–202.

Graham, D.J. & Hambrey, M.J. 2007. Sediments and landforms in an upland glaciated-valley landsystem: upper Ennerdale, English Lake District. In: Hambrey, M.J., Christoffersen, P., Glasser, N.F. & Hubbard, B. (eds), *Glacial sedimentary processes and products*. IAG Special Publication 39, Blackwell, Oxford, 235–256.

Gresswell, R.K. 1952. The glacial geomorphology of the south-eastern part of the Lake District. *Geological Journal* 1, 57–70.

Gresswell, R.K. 1962. The glaciology of the Coniston basin. *Geological Journal* 3, 83–96.

Hay, T. 1934. The glaciology of the Ullswater area. *Geographical Journal* 84, 136–148.

Huddart, D. 1967. Deglaciation in the Ennerdale area – a re-interpretation. *Proceedings, Cumberland Geological Society* 2, 63–75.

Lamb, A.L. & Ballantyne, C.K. 1998. Palaeonunataks and the altitude of the last ice sheet in the SW Lake District, England. *Proceedings of the Geologists' Association* 109, 305–316.

Manley, G. 1959. The late-glacial climate of north-west England. *Liverpool and Manchester Geological Journal* 2, 188–215.

McDougall, D.A. 2001. The geomorphological impact of Loch Lomond (Younger Dryas) Stadial plateau icefields in the central Lake District, north-west England. *Journal of Quaternary Science* 16, 531–543.

Raistrick, A. 1925. The glaciation of Borrowdale, Cumberland. *Proceedings of the Yorkshire Geological Society* 20, 155–181.

Sissons, J.B. 1980. The Loch Lomond Advance in the Lake District, northern England. *Transactions of the Royal Society of Edinburgh: Earth Sciences* 71, 13–27.

Smith, R.A. 1967. The deglaciation of south-west Cumberland: a reappraisal of some features in the Eskdale and Bootle areas. *Proceedings, Cumberland Geological Society* 2, 76–83.

Smith, R.A. 2008. *The Ice Age in the Lake District*. Rigg Side Publications, Keswick.

Swift, D. 1998. Origin and significance of a Late Devensian meltwater channel system near Aughtertree Fell, northern Cumbria. *Proceedings, Cumberland Geological Society* 6, 183–201.

Temple, P.H. 1965. Some aspects of cirque distribution in the west-central Lake District, northern England. *Geografiska Annaler* 47A, 185–193.

Walker, D. 1966. The glaciation of the Langdale fells. *Geological Journal* 5, 208–215.

Wilson, P. 1977. The Rosthwaite moraines. *Proceedings, Cumberland Geological Society* 3, 239–249.

Wilson, P. 1982. Drumlins at Watendlath. *Proceedings, Cumberland Geological Society* 4, 105–110.

Wilson, P. 2002. Morphology and significance of some Loch Lomond Stadial moraines in the south-central Lake District, England. *Proceedings of the Geologists' Association* 113, 9–21.

Wilson, P. 2004. Implications of dissected drift at Stockdale Head, western Lake District. *Geological Journal* 39, 111–115.

Wilson, P. 2004. Description and implications of valley moraines in upper Eskdale, Lake District. *Proceedings of the Geologists' Association* 115, 55–61.

Wilson, P. & Clark, R. 1998. Characteristics and implications of some Loch Lomond Stadial moraine ridges and later landforms, eastern Lake District, northern England. *Geological Journal* 33, 73–87.

Wilson, P. & Clark, R. 1999. Further glacier and snowbed sites of inferred Loch Lomond Stadial age in the northern Lake District. *Proceedings of the Geologists' Association* 110, 321–331.

Periglacial landforms

Allison, R.J. & Davies, K.C. 1996. Ploughing boulders as evidence of down-slope sediment transport in the English Lake District. *Zeitschrift für Geomorphologie, Supplement-Band* 106, 199–219.

Ballantyne, C.K. & Kirkbride, M.P. 1986. The characteristics and significance of some Lateglacial protalus ramparts in upland Britain. *Earth Surface Processes and Landforms* 11, 659–671.

Boardman, J. 1977. Stratified screes in the northern Lake District. *Proceedings, Cumberland Geological Society* 3, 233–237.

Boardman, J. 1978. Grèzes litées near Keswick. *Biuletyn Peryglacjalny* 27, 23–34.

Boardman, J. 1985. The northeastern Lake District: periglacial slope deposits. In: Boardman, J. (ed.), *Field guide to the periglacial landforms of northern England*. Quaternary Research Association, Cambridge, 23–37.

Caine, T.N. 1963. The origin of sorted stripes in the Lake District, northern England. *Geografiska Annaler* 65A, 172–179.

Caine, T.N. 1963. Movement of low angle scree slopes in the Lake District, northern England. *Revue de Géomorphologie Dynamique* 14, 171–177.

Caine, N. 1974. The distribution of sorted patterned ground in the English Lake District. *Revue de Géomorphologie Dynamique* 21, 49–56.

Hay, T. 1936. Stones stripes. *Geographical Journal* 87, 47–50

Hollingworth, S.E. 1934. Some solifluction phenomena in the northern part of the Lake District. *Proceedings of the Geologists' Association* 45, 167–188.

Oxford, S.P. 1985. Protalus ramparts, protalus rock glaciers and solifluction till in the northwest part of the English Lake District. In: Boardman, J. (ed.), *Field guide to the periglacial landforms of northern England*. Quaternary Research Association, Cambridge, 38–46.

Oxford, S.P. 1994. Periglacial snowbed landforms at Dead Crags, Cumbria. In: Boardman, J. & Walden, J. (eds), *The Quaternary of Cumbria: field guide*. Quaternary Research Association, Oxford, 158–164.

Tufnell, L. 1966. Some little-studied British landforms. *Proceedings, Cumberland Geological Society* 2, 50–56.

Tufnell, L. 1969. The range of periglacial phenomena in northern England. *Biuletyn Peryglacjalny* 19, 291–323.

Warburton, J. 1985. Contemporary patterned ground (sorted stripes) in the Lake District. In: Boardman, J. (ed.), *Field guide to the periglacial landforms of northern England*. Quaternary Research Association, Cambridge, 54–62.

Warburton, J. 1987. Characteristic ratios of width to depth-of-sorting for sorted stripes in the English Lake District. In: Boardman, J. (ed.), *Periglacial processes and landforms in Britain and Ireland*. Cambridge University Press, Cambridge, 163–171.

Warburton, J. 1997. Patterned ground in the Lake District. In: Boardman, J. (ed.), *Geomorphology of the Lake District: a field guide.* British Geomorphological Research Group, Oxford, 107–119.

Warburton, J. & Caine, N. 1999. Sorted patterned ground in the English Lake District. *Permafrost and Periglacial Processes* 10, 193–197.

Whalley, B. 1997. Protalus ramparts, rock glaciers and protalus lobes in the Lake District. In: Boardman, J. (ed.), *Geomorphology of the Lake District: a field guide.* British Geomorphological Research Group, Oxford, 51–61.

Wilson, P. 1993. Ploughing-boulder characteristics and associated soil properties in the Lake District and southern Scotland. *Scottish Geographical Magazine* 109, 18–26.

Hillslope landforms

Andrews, J.T. 1961. The development of scree slopes in the English Lake District and central Quebec-Labrador. *Cahers de Geographie de Quebec* 10, 219–230.

Brook, M.S. & Tippett, J.M. 2002. The influence of rock mass strength on the form and evolution of deglaciated valley slopes in the English Lake District. *Scottish Journal of Geology* 38, 15–20.

Clark, R. & Wilson, P. 2004. A rock avalanche deposit in Burtness Comb, Lake District, northwest England. *Geological Journal* 39, 419–430.

Hay, T. 1935. Scree with great boulders. *Geographical Journal* 85, 372–375.

Melville, C. 1986. Historical earthquakes in northwest England. *Transactions of the Cumberland and Westmorland Antiquarian and Archaeological Society* 86, 193–219.

Smith, R.A. 2002. The Bowder Stone, Grange-in-Borrowdale, Cumbria. *Proceedings, Cumberland Geological Society* 6, 525–539.

Warburton, J., Milledge, D. & Johnson, R. 2008. Assessment of shallow landslide activity following the January 2005 storm, northern Cumbria. *Proceedings, Cumberland Geological Society* 7, 263–283

Wilson, P. 2003. Landslides in Lakeland. *Conserving Lakeland* 40, 24–25.

Wilson, P. 2005. Paraglacial rock-slope failures in Wasdale, western Lake District, England: morphology, styles and significance. *Proceedings of the Geologists' Association* 116, 349–361.

Wilson, P., Clark, R. & Smith, A. 2004. Rock-slope failures in the Lake District: a preliminary report. *Proceedings, Cumberland Geological Society* 7, 13–36.

Wilson, P. & Smith, A. 2006. Geomorphological characteristics and significance of Late Quaternary paraglacial rock-slope failures on Skiddaw Group terrain, Lake District, northwest England. *Geografiska Annaler* 88A, 237–252.

Rivers, Lakes and Tarns

Boardman, J. 1997. The terraces of Mosedale Beck: a review. In: Boardman, J. (ed.), *Geomorphology of the Lake District: a field guide*. British Geomorphological Research Group, Oxford, 7–9.

Boardman, J. & Smith, R. 1994. The Seathwaite valley. In: Boardman, J. & Walden, J. (eds), *The Quaternary of Cumbria: field guide*. Quaternary Research Association, Oxford, 143–145.

Carling, P. 1997. Sedimentology of the 1749 flood deposit. In: Boardman, J. (ed.), *Geomorphology of the Lake District: a field guide*. British Geomorphological Research Group, Oxford, 23–29.

Chiverrell, R.C., Harvey, A.M. & Foster, G.C. 2007. Hillslope gullying in the Solway Firth – Morecambe Bay region, Great Britain: responses to human impact and/or climatic deterioration. *Geomorphology* 84, 317–343.

Clark, R., Parker, A.G., Anderson, D.E. & Wilson, P. 2007. Late Holocene debris cone development and vegetation and land-use history in the Pasture Beck valley, Lake District, NW England. *Proceedings of the Yorkshire Geological Society* 56, 235–243.

Harvey, A.M. 1997. Fluvial geomorphology of north-west England. In: Gregory, K.J. (ed.), *Fluvial geomorphology of Great Britain*. Chapman & Hall, London.

Haworth, E., de Boer, G., Evans, I., Osmaston, H., Pennington, W., Smith, A., Story, P. & Ware, B. 2003. *Tarns of the central Lake District*. Brathay Exploration Group Trust, Ambleside.

Hay, T. 1926. Delta formation in the English Lakes. *Geological Magazine* 63, 292–301.

Hay, T. 1928. The shore topography of the English Lakes. *Geographical Journal* 72, 38–57.

Hay, T. 1928. Glenridding flood of 1927. *Geographical Journal* 73, 90–91.

Hay, T. 1930. Further notes on the shore topography of the English Lakes. *Geographical Journal* 75, 324–344.

Johnson, R.M. & Warburton, J. 2002. Flooding and geomorphic impacts in a mountain torrent: Raise Beck, central Lake District, England. *Earth Surface Processes and Landforms* 27, 945–969.

Johnson, R.M. & Warburton, J. 2002. Annual sediment budget of a UK mountain torrent. *Geografiska Annaler* 84A, 73–88.

Johnson, R.M. & Warburton, J. 2003. Regional assessment of contemporary debris-flow activity in Lake District mountain catchments, northern England: occurrence, scale and process. In: Rickenmann, D. & Chen, C-L. (eds) *Debris-flow hazards mitigation: mechanics, prediction and assessment*. Millpress, Rotterdam, 965–976.

Johnson, R.M. & Warburton, J. 2006. Variability in sediment supply, transfer and deposition in an upland torrent system: Iron Crag, northern England. *Earth Surface Processes and Landforms* 31, 844–861.

Marr, J.E. 1895. The tarns of Lakeland. *Quarterly Journal of the Geological Society* 51, 35–48.

Mitchell, G.H. 1931. The pre-glacial history of the River Kent, Westmorland. *Proceedings of the Liverpool Geological Society* 15, 78–83.

Parker, A.G., Anderson, D.E. & Boardman, J. 1994. Seathwaite valley: buried organic deposit. In: Boardman, J. & Walden, J. (eds), *The Quaternary of Cumbria: field guide*. Quaternary Research Association, Oxford, 146–151.

Smith, A. 1996. Alluvial fans in the Buttermere-Crummock valley. *Proceedings, Cumberland Geological Society* 6, 47–62.

Van Duzer, C. 2004. *Floating Islands: A global bibliography, with an edition and translation of G. C. Munz's 'Exercitatio academica de insulis natantibus' (1711)*. Cantor Press, Los Altos Hills.

Limestone landforms

Vincent, P. 1995. Limestone pavements in the British Isles: a review. *Geographical Journal* 161, 265–274.

Vincent, P. 1996. Rillenkarren in the British Isles. *Zeitschrift für Geomorphologie* 40, 487–497.

Vincent, P. 2004. Polygenetic origin of limestone pavements in northern England. *Zeitschrift für Geomorphologie* 48, 481–490.

Vincent, P. & Lee, M.J. 1981. Some observations on the loess around Morecambe Bay, north-west England. *Proceedings of the Yorkshire Geological Society* 43, 281–294.

Societies

T HERE ARE SEVERAL SOCIETIES that concern themselves
either wholly or in part with the geology and geomorphology of
the Lake District. They are:

- **The Cumberland Geological Society:** founded in 1962, concentrates on geology in the county of Cumbria and the Lake District.
- **The Westmorland Geological Society:** founded in 1973, focuses on the geology of the area around Kendal.
- **The Yorkshire Geological Society:** founded in 1837, covers geological themes in Northern England.

Each society holds summer field meetings and winter lectures.

In addition, the **Quaternary Research Association** and the **British Society for Geomorphology** have held field meetings in the Lake District.

All these organisations are open to professionals and amateurs. Membership details and benefits for each society can be found on their web sites.

Index